Bible

stories

for

Jewish children

from Joshua to Queen Esther

by RUTH SAMUELS

Illustrated by LASZLO MATULAY

KTAV PUBLISHING HOUSE INC.

Design and Art Supervision by EZEKIEL SCHLOSS

Table of Contents

Joshua Sends Spies Into Canaan

After the death of Moses, Joshua became the leader of Israel.

He led the people across the Jordan River and into the Promised Land.

But Joshua knew that the Children of Israel could not yet claim the Promised Land for their own. They would have to fight before the land could be won.

One day, he called the people together and said:

"Before the Promised Land can really be ours, we must capture the city of Jericho. It is a very wicked city and great walls have been built around it. I must send spies to Jericho to find out how strong the walls are and how great an army the king of Jericho has."

"I will go to Jericho!" cried one brave man.

"And I!" cried another.

Were the walls of Jericho high or low?
That was what Joshua wanted to know.
Then two of his brave men cried, "Let us go!
"We'll bring back the news about Jericho!"

The next morning, the two spies began their journey.

When they reached Jericho, they saw that the walls around the city were high and wide. The gates of the city were open. The spies pretended to be shepherds and walked past the guards and through the city gates.

When night came, they stopped at an inn, owned by a kind woman named Rahab.

Suddenly, there came a loud knock at the door of the inn.

"Come out, spies from Israel!" cried a voice.

"It is our soldiers!" whispered Rahab. "Go up to the roof and hide," she said to the men from Israel.

As the men hurried up the ladder, Rahab opened the door of the inn.

Two soldiers stood outside.

"Where are the two men who came here tonight?" they asked.

"They left as soon as they ate their supper," said Rahab.

The soldiers hurried away, and Rahab climbed the ladder to the roof. She found the two spies hiding under some bundles of flax. Rahab then showed the men a red cord that hung from the roof to the road below.

"Slide down this cord," she said, "and leave the city as fast as you can!"

The two spies thanked this kind woman for all she had done.

"When our soldiers march into Jericho," they said, "hang this red cord from your window. When our men see it, they will do you no harm, for they will know that in this house lives a brave woman who helped Israel."

Then the two men slid down the red cord and fled from the city.

The soldiers of Jericho searched high and low but never found them.

The spies hid in the mountains for three days and then returned to camp to tell Joshua about the walls of Jericho.

Israel Crosses the Jordan

All was quiet in the camp of the Israelites. It was night time, and the people slept peacefully in their tents. Not far from the camp, the River Jordan wound through the land like a silver ribbon.

On the bank of the river stood a man. It was Joshua, new leader of Israel. For Moses had died when he was one hundred and twenty years old. Before Moses died, God spoke to him and said:

"Choose Joshua to take your place."

Now Joshua stood gazing across the Jordan at the green fields and rich vineyards of the Promised Land. The air was sweet with the fragrance of ripe fruit and wonderful flowers.

"It is indeed a land of milk and honey," thought Joshua. "But alas! It will never be ours. For how can we cross this great wide river!"

Suddenly, in the still of the night, Joshua heard a voice:

"Be strong and of good courage!" said the voice.

Joshua knew this was the voice of God.

"Tomorrow Israel will cross the Jordan," said God. "Send the Holy Ark before you, and fear not, for I shall be with you as I was with Moses."

After three days of preparations, Joshua said to the people:

"Today we cross the Jordan. Do not fear, for God is with us, just as He was with our people when they fled from Egypt and crossed the Red Sea with Moses."

Then Joshua told the priests to take up the Holy Ark and lead the way.

Lo and behold! When the priests stepped into the river, the waters of the Jordan parted and a path of dry land led to the other side.

The Children of Israel shouted with joy. But some of the old people wept, for they remembered all those who had died in the wilderness and would never see this wonderful land.

The priests stood in the middle of the river with the Holy Ark, while the people crossed over to the other side.

The Holy Ark it led the way
Across the Jordan wide.
While Israel, with the help of God,
Crossed to the other side.

After everyone had crossed the river, God told Joshua to select twelve men, one from each tribe. Joshua said to them: "Go down into the river and bring up from it twelve stones, as large stones as you can carry, from the place where the priests are standing." He placed the stones on the shore.

"Whoever sees those stones," he said, "will know that God was with the Children of Israel when they crossed the Jordan."

After the priests had carried the Holy Ark up out of the river, the waters came together, and the Jordan flowed on its way again through the Land of Canaan.

The Walls of Jericho

Two men were walking along the road that led from Jericho to the camp of the Israelites. The men walked slowly, for they were weak from hunger.

These men were the two spies that Joshua, leader of Israel, had sent to Jericho.

When the people of Israel saw the spies returning they sent up a great cheer. Then they all began to ask questions at once.

"Wait!" commanded Joshua. "Let the men eat and drink first! Then they will tell us their news."

After the two men had eaten and rested, Joshua asked them what they had found out.

"The walls of Jericho are high and wide," said the spies, "but they are cracked in many places. The soldiers are fat and lazy."

That night, Joshua sat in his tent, trying to think of a plan for capturing Jericho. Then, he heard a voice say:

"March once around the city of Jericho with the Holy Ark. Tell the priests to blow hard upon their rams horns. Do this every day for six days. On the seventh day, march seven times around the city. When the priests blow upon their horns and the people shout with all their might, the walls of Jericho will fall."

Joshua knew this was the voice of God.

The next morning, Joshua called the people together.

"Today we march on Jericho!" he said.

"God has told me how we can capture the city."

The Children of Israel marched along the road to Jericho. When the king of Jericho heard the sound of the marching feet, he ordered his soldiers to lock the city gates.

Once around the walls of Jericho marched the Children of Israel, with the Holy Ark leading the way.

"Halt!" cried Joshua.

Then he raised his hand. The priests blew so hard upon their rams' horns that the people in the city thought the sky would surely fall.

Every day, for six days, the Children of Israel marched once around the walls of Jericho.

On the seventh day, they marched seven times around the city.

Then such a sound went up as was never heard before.

The priests blew upon their horns and every man of Israel shouted with all his might.

With a tumbling and a rumbling, the walls of Jericho came down!

Seven times around the great walls
Marched the Children of Israel.
The trumpets blew, the voices roared,
Til the walls of Jericho fell!

The soldiers of Israel rushed into the city and burned it to the ground—all but the house where a red cord hung from a window. This was the house of Rahab, the kind woman who had helped the two spies.

"With the help of God, we have captured Jericho," said the people of Israel. "Now the Promised Land is really ours!"

The Sun Stood Still

With Joshua as their brave new leader, the Children of Israel had captured the city of Jericho, and had made peace with the people of Gibeon, a nearby country.

Late one night, Joshua was awakened from his sleep by the sound of loud talking outside his tent. He heard a strange man's voice ask:

"Where is Joshua, leader of Israel?"

Joshua stepped outside his tent. He saw two strangers talking to some of his soldiers.

"Who comes riding into our camp at this late hour?" asked Joshua.

"We are men of Gibeon," said one of the strangers. "Our king has sent us to ask your help. The Ammorites are marching against us with their great armies. Will you come and save us?"

"We will march at once," said Joshua.

All that night, the brave soldiers of Israel marched. As they came near Gibeon, they saw a man on horseback riding swiftly out to meet them. It was the king of Gibeon.

"Last night the Ammorites attacked us," he cried. "But a strange thing happened.

Hail and rain fell from the sky and almost destroyed their camp. But not one drop of rain or one hailstone fell upon us."

"That means the Lord is with us," said Joshua.

Then he turned to his men and cried:

"We will march against the Ammorites at once!"

The soldiers of Israel fought the Ammorites with such skill that they soon drove the enemy soldiers deep into the hills.

But Joshua knew the battle was not yet won. For as he looked at the western sky, he saw that the sun would soon go down.

"When it is dark we will not be able to see the enemy," he thought, "and they will shoot their arrows at us from the caves in the hills. If only I could hold back the sun for just a few hours!"

Joshua raised his arms to the sky.

"Oh, God of Israel," he cried, "hear my prayer!"

Hold back the night and stop the sun;
Let there be light for Israel
Until the battle we have won!"
Then every eye turned to the sky,
For lo! The sun stood still on high.

The soldiers of Israel gazed at the sun with wonder. Then they gave a great shout.

"The Lord is with us!" they cried. They rushed upon the Ammorites with such force that the enemy was soon defeated.

When the battle was over, the sun went down behind the hills.

"Let us give thanks to God," said Joshua.

In the soft light of the moon, the soldiers of Israel bowed their heads in prayer.

The Songs of Deborah

For many years, Joshua was a wise leader of Israel. But after his death, there was no great leader to take his place. The people forgot about God and began to worship idols.

When the wicked king of Canaan saw how weak the people of Israel had become, he said, "Now is my chance to drive these people out of the land. I will send my great army to attack them."

At that time, in the hill country of Ephraim, there lived a very brave prophetess and judge named Deborah. Deborah used to sit under a palm tree near her home and sing about the glory of God and judge.

Now when the people of Ephraim heard that the king of Canaan was sending an army against Israel, they went to Deborah and said:

"What shall we do?"

"Israel must fight!" cried Deborah.

"But we have no leader!" said the people.

"I have heard that in the tribe of Naphtali there is a brave young man called Barak," said Deborah. "Let us send for him at once!"

A few days later, as Deborah sat beneath the palm tree, a young man came and stood before her.

"I am Barak," he said. "Why did you send for me?"

"I have heard of your great courage," said Deborah. "Can you lead an army of ten thousand men against the armies of the king of Canaan?"

"But the king's armies are led by Sisera," said Barak. "His men ride in chariots of iron. Even ten thousand soldiers would be helpless against them."

"But iron chariots cannot climb a mountain," said Deborah. "If you lead your men to the top of Mount Tabor, you can rush down upon Sisera's soldiers and defeat them."

"A very wise plan," said Barak. "I will do what you ask. But only if you come with me."

"I, a woman, go into battle!" cried Deborah.

"No man of Israel will want anyone to think a woman is braver than he," said Barak. "When the men hear you are going with me, they will not dare refuse to fight."

"Very well," said Deborah, "I will go with you."

The news went from tribe to tribe that Deborah was going into battle, and every man of Israel cried:

"If a woman is brave enough, so am I!"

Barak soon had his army, and ten thousand strong they marched to the top of Mount Tabor.

When Sisera's iron chariots came thundering across the valley, they could go no farther than the foot of the mountain.

Barak's men rushed down upon them with such force that the enemy was soon defeated.

After the battle, Deborah sat once more beneath the palm tree.

"Oh, people of all other lands," she sang,
Hear now our song of victory!
Once more the mighty Israel
Becomes a nation, proud and free!

For forty years after this, the people of Israel lived in peace.

Gideon Breaks the Idols

Great trouble had come to the Children of Israel. The wild men of Midian were stealing their grain and burning their houses. The people were fleeing into the hills to live in caves.

But there was one brave young man who did not fear the men of Midian. His name was Gideon. Gideon planted his grain and guarded his fields day and night.

One day, as Gideon was ploughing his field, a man came and stood before him. The man had a very kind and gentle face.

"Who are you?" Gideon asked.

"The Lord has sent me," said the man.

"How can I be sure you come from the Lord?"

The man told him to put some food on a rock nearby. He touched the food with his staff, and fire flashed out of the rock.

Then Gideon knew this was an angel of the Lord.

"Your people are filled with fear," said the angel. "They have forgotten God and worship idols of wood and stone. You must help them."

Then the angel went away.

"What can I do?" thought Gideon sadly.

"My own father has built an altar to Baal and Ashtoreth, the false gods."

That night, as Gideon lay sleeping, he heard the voice of God say:

"Arise, Gideon, and destroy your father's altar!"

The next morning, Gideon called together ten of his trusted friends.

"Tonight I shall destroy my father's altar," he told them. "Will you help me?"

"We may be killed!" cried the young men.

"The Lord will be with us!" said Gideon.

In the dark and still of night, Gideon and his friends threw down the altar of Baal and smashed it to pieces.

Gideon struck with all his might
And the altar of Baal fell.
Then Gideon offered up a prayer,
To the true God of Israel.

The next morning, Gideon's father told all the men of the city that someone had destroyed his altar. The men began to search for the guilty person. Then the news was whispered about that Gideon had broken the altar.

The men of the city went to Gideon's father.

"Bring out your son!" they cried, "for he is guilty and we shall kill him!"

"My son risked his life for the God of Israel!" cried Gideon's father. "But how many of you would die for Baal? And if he is such a powerful god, why doesn't he punish Gideon?"

When the men heard this, they were ashamed. They asked God to forgive them for worshiping foolish idols.

The Trumpets and the Pitchers

When the people of Israel heard that Gideon had destroyed the altar to Baal, their hearts were filled with new hope.

"Once again Israel has a brave leader!" they cried.

Then came the news that the Midianites and the Amalekites were coming with thousands of soldiers to attack the people of Israel.

Gideon sent out a message, asking the men of Israel to join his army.

Thirty-two thousand men answered his call. They marched behind Gideon to the foot of Mount Gilead.

But as Gideon watched his men making camp, his heart grew troubled. Many of these soldiers were young boys. Others were old men.

"How can I send them out to be killed in battle?" Gideon thought.

Then he heard the voice of God say:

"Send back home the men who are not trained to fight. Take the others to the river to drink. Some of the men will lap the water like dogs. Take only these men into battle."

The next day, Gideon sent the young boys and old men back home. He took the men who were left to the river. Only three hundred of them drank like dogs. These men Gideon kept for his army.

That night, Gideon and his servant went to spy upon the enemy. They hid in the shadows near the enemy camp and listened to the soldiers talking.

"Last night," said one soldier, "I dreamed a cake of barley came rolling into our camp and knocked down a tent!"

"That means Gideon of Israel will come into our camp and defeat us," said another man.

When Gideon heard these words, he whispered to his servant:

"Let us hurry back to camp, for now is the time to attack!"

Gideon divided his three hundred men into three companies. He gave each man a horn and a pitcher. In each pitcher was a lighted torch.

Still as mice, Gideon's army marched through the night. Just outside the enemy camp, they halted. Not a sound could be heard but the snores of the sleeping enemy soldiers. Suddenly, Gideon gave a loud blast on his horn. This was the signal! The men of Israel charged into the enemy camp!

With pitchers crashing and torches flashing,
Israel charged on Midian.
The trumpets blew, the voices cried,
"For the Lord and for Gideon!"

The sleeping enemy thought the end of the world had come! They were so frightened, they began to run as fast as they could. On and on they ran, until they had reached their own land.

After this great victory, the people of Israel left the caves in the hills and went back to their homes. But when they asked Gideon to be their ruler, he said:

"Israel has but one ruler, and He is the Lord."

Samson, The Strong Man

Once there lived a man called Manoah. He owned much land and many herds of cattle and sheep. Manoah had a beautiful wife, but he and his wife were very unhappy, for they had no children.

Every day, Manoah's wife went into the fields to pray for a son. One day, as she was kneeling in prayer, an angel came and spoke to her.

"God will give you a son," said the angel. "But remember this: you must never cut your son's hair. He will be very strong and become a great leader."

Manoah's wife wept for joy and ran to tell her husband this wonderful news.

One day, a beautiful baby son was born to Manoah and his wife. They called the baby Samson.

When Samson became a man, he was very strong. His hair was long and thick for never once had it been cut. One day, as Samson walked along a mountain path, a lion sprang out at him. Samson killed the lion with his bare hands. Soon all the people of Israel were talking of Samson and his great strength.

Now at this time, Israel lived under the rule of the wicked Philistines. The Philistines had taken land and vineyards from the people of Israel. Many of the people were starving. This made Samson very angry. One night, he tied lighted torches to the tails of three-hundred foxes. Then he set the foxes loose in the fields of the Philistines. The crops were burned to the ground.

When the Philistines found out that Samson had done this, they cried:

"We must capture this mighty man of Israel and kill him!"

Samson hid in a cave, deep in the mountains. The Philistines called together an army of three thousand men to capture him. When the people of Israel saw all these soldiers, they were afraid.

"We will bring Samson to you ourselves," they told the lords of the Philistines. Then the people went to the cave where Samson was hiding.

"Please give yourself up," they begged him, "or the Philistines will make Israel suffer more than ever."

Samson loved his people very much, so he let them tie him with ropes and lead him to the Philistines.

But when Samson saw the cruel faces of the Philistine leaders, his heart was filled with rage. On the ground before him he saw the jawbone of an ass. Samson picked it up, and swinging right and left, he killed a thousand Philistines. Then, panting with thirst, he cried:

"Water! Lord, give me water!"

Lo and behold! From out of a rock nearby came a stream of clear, cold water.

"It is a miracle!" the people cried. "Truly this man is sent to us by the Lord!"

With the jawbone of an ass
Samson slew a thousand men.
The people watched with wonder
For he had the strength of ten.

Samson and Delilah

Samson, the strong man, had been a wise judge of Israel for many years. The leaders of the Philistines hated Samson, for he would not let them take land and cattle from his people.

"If only we could find out what makes Samson strong," said the Philistines, "we could capture him."

Now Samson had fallen in love with a beautiful Philistine woman named Delilah. Delilah was very greedy and loved fine clothes and jewels more than anything in the world.

One day, the leaders of the Philistines came to Delilah and said:

"If you will find out the secret of Samson's great strength, we will give you eleven hundred pieces of silver."

That evening, as Delilah and Samson were dining, Delilah smiled her prettiest smile and said:

"Tell me, Samson, what makes you so strong?"

Samson's eyes twinkled.

"Tie me up with seven fresh bowstrings," he said, "and I will become weak."

But when Delilah had bound him with the bowstrings, Samson broke them with one twist of his mighty arms.

Delilah's eyes filled with angry tears.

"You are teasing me!" she cried.

"Please don't cry," said Samson. "I will tell you my secret. I am strong because my hair has never been cut. But you must promise to tell no one!"

"I promise!" said Delilah. Then she gave Samson a glass of strong wine to drink and he fell into a deep sleep. Delilah hurried to the leaders of the Philistines.

"Come quickly!" she cried, "and cut off Samson's hair. Then he will be weak as any man!"

After Samson's hair had been cut, he was too weak to raise his hand.

The cruel Philistines threw him into prison and put out both his eyes.

The days passed, and as Samson lay in prison, his hair began to grow again.

One day, the Philistines were having a feast in the temple of their false god, Dagon.

"Let us bring Samson here," said one of the leaders. "It will be great fun for the people to see how weak he has become!"

Samson was led to the temple between two prison guards. The Philistines shouted with laughter at his ragged clothes and thin body.

But when Samson heard their shouts, he was filled with rage.

"Let me stand between two pillars of the temple," he said to his guards.

With a hand on each tall pillar
Samson stood before the great throng.
He raised his blind eyes to the skies
And cried, "Oh, God, please make me strong!"

Then he pushed with all his might!

With a noise like thunder, the temple of the false god came crashing down. The screaming Philistines were buried beneath it. Alas, poor Samson died with them. He had given his life for Israel.

Ruth and Naomi

Long ago, in the land of Moab, there lived a woman called Naomi. Great trouble had come to Naomi, for death had taken her husband and her two fine sons. Naomi's two daughters-in-law, Ruth and Orpah, were very kind and tried to cheer the older woman, even though their own hearts ached with grief.

But the three women had no men to care for them and they were very poor. One day, as Naomi sat weeping, Ruth said to her:

"Please do not weep, mother, for you still have Orpah and me and we love you dearly."

Naomi dried her tears and said:

"Yes, I am blessed with two fine daughters-in-law. But I am lonely for my own people in Judah. Ten years ago, my husband and I came here because there was a terrible famine in our own land. But now I want to go back home."

"We will go with you," said Ruth and Orpah. But Naomi shook her head.

"No," she said, "you are still young and must go back to your own people. As time passes, your hearts will grow light again. You will find good husbands and have fine sons."

Orpah kissed Naomi goodbye tenderly and went back to her own people. But Ruth would not leave Naomi, for she knew her mother-in-law needed someone to care for her.

"Do not tell me to go home, mother," said Ruth, "for where you go, I will go also. Your people will be my people and your God my God."

To Naomi, did Ruth make this vow:
"Your people will my people be.
Wherever you go—I will follow you.
Your God will be my God, too."

At these words, Naomi's eyes filled with tears and she kissed Ruth tenderly.

"My own daughter could not love me more," she said.

The next morning, Ruth and Naomi began their journey to the town of Bethlehem in Judah. But when they reached Bethlehem, they were very tired and hungry.

"You should not have come with me," said Naomi sadly, "for here we may starve."

"No, mother, we will not starve," said Ruth. "The men in the fields are reaping the barley harvest. I will go and join the gleaners and bring home plenty of food for us both."

In those long-ago days, the poor people followed behind the reapers in the fields and picked up the grain that was left behind on the ground. These people were called gleaners.

Ruth went to join the gleaners in the fields of a rich man called Boaz. All day she followed behind the reapers, and that night she returned home with her arms full of grain. Naomi wept for joy when Ruth showed her how much grain she had gathered.

"God has not forgotten us," said Naomi. "Let us thank Him for sending us this food."

Ruth and Boaz

It was harvest time in Judah. Near the city of Bethlehem there were many fields of barley owned by a very rich man called Boaz. Now the reapers were busy in these fields, gathering the sheaves of grain. Behind the reapers came the gleaners. The gleaners were poor people who were allowed to pick up the grain that the reapers left behind.

One of the gleaners in the fields of Boaz was a young woman with a sweet face and beautiful dark eyes. One day Boaz came to look over his fields. He noticed the pretty young woman and said to one of the reapers:

"Who is that woman and why is it that she must gather grain with the poor?"

"Her name is Ruth," said the reaper. "She came to Bethlehem a short time ago from the land of Moab, with her mother-in-law, Naomi."

"Naomi!" cried Boaz. "I had a kinsman who married a woman called Naomi. They had two sons and ten years ago they left here to go to Moab."

"Naomi must be your kinswoman," said the reaper, "for she, too, had two sons. Her husband and her sons are now dead and she is very poor. It is said that her daughter-in-law, Ruth, cares for her as if Naomi were her own mother."

"Tell this woman I wish to speak with her," said Boaz.

When Ruth stood before him, Boaz said:

"Your mother-in-law, Naomi, is my kinswoman. I have heard of your kindness to her. You may gather grain in my fields as long as you wish. If you like, you may eat your meals with the reapers."

Ruth's lovely eyes filled with tears of joy as she thanked Boaz for his kindness. After she had gone back to the fields, Boaz said to the reapers:

"Leave plenty of grain behind so that Ruth may have all she needs."

From that day on, Boaz came every day to the field where Ruth gathered grain, for he could not forget her lovely, sweet face. Then one day Boaz asked Ruth to become his wife, for he had fallen deeply in love with her. Naomi was filled with joy when Ruth told her this happy news.

"God has led us to this place," she said.

Ruth and Boaz were married and lived together happily all of their lives. One of their fine grandsons was Jesse, who was the father of David, the great king of Israel.

"I will gather barley, mother,"
Ruth to Naomi said.
"So you can grind it into meal,
And bake us loaves of bread."

The Birth of Samuel

Eli, the priest, stood in the doorway of the temple of Shiloh.

All day long, the people had come from miles around, bringing their yearly sacrifices to God. Eli was tired, but very happy, for he loved to see his people worshiping the Lord.

But suddenly, from inside the temple, came a strange sound.

"Can that be someone weeping?" thought Eli. He hurried into the temple. There before the altar knelt a woman, sobbing as if her heart would break.

"Who are you?" asked Eli, "and why do you weep?"

The woman raised her eyes. Her face was thin and sad.

"I am Hannah," she said. "Every day I pray for a son, but my prayers are not answered."

"Go home and weep no more," said Eli. "God will send you a son."

As Hannah looked into the kind eyes of the priest, her heart was filled with hope.

"When my son is born," she said, "I will bring him to you."

Another year passed, and again the people brought their sacrifices to the temple. Among those who came was a woman who carried a beautiful baby boy in her arms. She went to Eli and said:

"I have brought you my son."

Eli could hardly believe his eyes. The woman was Hannah, but how she had changed! Her cheeks were like roses and her eyes sparkled with joy.

Hannah put her son in Eli's arms.

"His name is Samuel," she said. "Keep him here and teach him to serve the Lord."

The baby Samuel grew to be a fine, handsome boy. Eli loved him as a son. Eli had sons of his own, but they were wicked men. Many times they would steal the gifts the people left on the altar of God.

One night, Eli lay on his bed, thinking sadly of his sons.

"Alas!" thought the old priest, "who will take my place when I die?"

Suddenly, he saw Samuel standing in the doorway.

"I heard a voice call my name," said Samuel.

"I heard no voice," said Eli. "It must have been the voice of God. If you hear it again, you must answer."

Samuel went back to his cot inside the temple. Again he heard a voice call his name. The boy trembled with fear and wonder.

"Speak, Lord," he whispered. "Your servant listens."

"The House of Eli will be destroyed," said the voice of God.

"Eli, Eli, who calls my name?"
Asked the young lad Samuel.
"I did not call," the old priest said.
"'Twas the God of Israel!"

The next morning, Samuel told Eli what God had said.

The old priest gave Samuel his blessing and said:

"Now I know you are the one to take my place."

As the years passed, Samuel became a great prophet in Israel. The people came from near and far to hear him speak the word of God.

Samuel, Leader of Israel

In the land of Canaan, there was a town called Mizpah, built on the very top of a hill. The hill looked like a giant stairway, for the wind and rain had made steps in it from top to bottom.

To this place came the Children of Israel, to hear their beloved leader, Samuel, as he spoke the word of God. Such great crowds came to Mizpah that there was not enough room in the town for all the people. They sat on the steps on the hillside; while Samuel stood at the bottom of the hill, telling them about the great laws of Moses. Samuel told the people how wicked it was to have false gods. He taught them to worship again the God of Israel.

Into the city of Mizpah
The Children of Israel came.
They came by hundreds and thousands
So great was Samuel's fame.

Now when the wicked Philistines found out that the people of Israel were all gathered together at Mizpah, their leaders said:

"Now is our chance! While the Israelites are all in one place, we can send our army against them and kill them all at once!"

Soon the news reached the Children of Israel at Mizpah that the cruel Philistines were coming to attack them.

"What shall we do!" the people cried, trembling with fear.

"Do not be afraid," said Samuel quietly. "Let us ask God for help."

Samuel made a sacrifice to God and began to pray. Hour after hour he prayed.

Then, in the distance, the people heard the sound of thousands of marching feet. The sound grew louder and louder.

"The Philistines!" the people cried.

But Samuel did not even look up. His head was bowed in prayer.

The Philistine army made camp so close to Mizpah that the Israelites could see the smoke from the enemy camp fires.

"Shall we attack the Philistines now?" asked the soldiers of Israel.

"No!" said Samuel. "We will wait." Then he began to pray once more.

When morning came, Samuel still knelt in prayer.

Then, suddenly, from out the heavens came a terrible crash of thunder. The sky grew dark and the rain poured down like rivers. A great flood washed over the Philistine camp, carrying away their tents and drowning many of their soldiers.

When at last the rain stopped, Samuel said:

"Now is the time to attack!"

The men of Israel rushed bravely forward. They drove the Philistines back to their own land. Once again God had helped the Children of Israel defeat their cruel enemies.

For many years after this great victory, Samuel was a wise leader in Israel.

Saul Is Chosen King

The people of Israel had gathered together once more at Mizpah. But this time, they had not come to hear Samuel speak, but to speak for themselves:

"We want a king!" they cried. "Israel needs a king like other nations!"

"A king will make you his slaves," said Samuel.

But still the people shouted: "We want a king!"

Then, as Samuel knelt in prayer, he heard the voice of God say:

"Give the people a king, Samuel."

"Go back to your homes," Samuel told the people. "I will choose a king."

Then one day, two men came to Samuel's house. One of the men was tall and very handsome.

"I am Saul, son of Kish," he said to Samuel. "This is my servant. We are looking for the great seer."

"I am the seer," said Samuel. Then he looked deeply into Saul's eyes and said:

"You need worry no more, for your father's donkeys are found."

Saul looked at Samuel with great wonder.

"This man must indeed be a great seer," he thought, "for how else could he know I was hunting for my father's two lost donkeys?"

Samuel asked Saul and his servant to come into the house for supper.

When they stepped inside, Saul saw about thirty great men of Israel sitting at a feast table.

"Why does the seer ask me to sit down with these great men?" he wondered.

After the meal was over, Samuel asked Saul and his servant to stay overnight and rest. The next morning, as the two men were leaving, Samuel said to Saul:

"Tell your servant to walk ahead. I want to speak to you alone."

When the servant had walked ahead, Samuel put his hand on Saul's shoulder and said:

"My son, listen closely to these words, for they are the words of God."

Saul stood very still. He felt frightened, for Samuel's eyes seemed to shine with a strange light. The old man took a small jar of oil and poured it over Saul's head. Then he kissed Saul and tears filled his eyes as he said:

"You have been chosen by God and anointed to be king of Israel."

Saul, here is God's word to you:
Rule, as the Torah commands you to.
Judge in mercy, Live in kindness,
Walk in truth and rule in justice.

A Shepherd Boy Is Chosen King

On a peaceful hillside near Bethlehem, David, son of Jesse, watched his father's sheep. As he watched, he played sweet music on a small harp and sang joyful songs about God and His wonders. David's songs were so sweet that all the other shepherds came to listen.

How beautiful is the morning sky,
How glorious is our God on high.
Lord of all things on land and on sea,
Like a Good Shepherd, He cares for me.

David was a very brave boy, and always trusted in the Lord. One day, as he was walking along a mountain path, he saw a lion crouching to spring upon his sheep. David placed a stone in his sling, then swiftly he sent the stone flying through the air. It struck the lion and he fell dead.

But little did David dream as he watched his sheep in the quiet hills that something strange and wonderful was going to happen. For on that very day, Samuel, the great prophet, had come to Bethlehem to choose a new king for Israel. King Saul had become a bad and selfish king, and one night, Samuel heard the voice of God say:

"Samuel! Go to Bethlehem and choose a new king. When you arrive there, say you have come to make a sacrifice. Send for a man named Jesse to come to the sacrifice

with his sons. But remember, when you choose the king, look not only at his face, but into his heart as well!"

Samuel started on his journey. When he reached Bethlehem, the elders of the city came to greet him.

"I have come to make a sacrifice to the Lord," said Samuel. "Send for a man called Jesse to come and bring his sons."

Jesse came with his fine, handsome sons to meet the great prophet. Samuel saw that Eliab, Jesse's oldest son, was more handsome than all his brothers.

"Ah," thought Samuel, "here indeed is a man fit to be a king!"

Then the prophet remembered the words of God:

"Look into the man's heart as well, Samuel!"

"Do you have any other sons?" Samuel asked Jesse.

"Yes," said Jesse, "there is David, who is tending the sheep."

"Send for him," said Samuel.

"Go and tell David to come here at once," said Jesse to one of his sons.

And so David came to stand before the great prophet of Israel in his rough shepherd's clothes. But when Samuel looked deep into the boy's eyes, he saw great courage and sweetness there.

Then, as if in a dream, the prophet heard a voice say:

"This is the one, Samuel!"

Samuel filled a horn with holy oil and poured it over the young boy's head.

And so David the shepherd boy was anointed king of Israel.

David and Goliath

On a quiet hillside in Bethlehem, David the shepherd boy watched his sheep and sang sweet songs about the Lord and the beautiful world. David was such a sweet singer that he had been asked many times to come and sing for King Saul of Israel, to cheer him when he was sad.

But now David wished he were with his brothers, who were with King Saul's army, fighting the Philistines.

Then one day, David's father gave him a package and said:

"Here is some good bread and cheese and some grain for your brothers. Take it to them at once."

Saul's army was camped on top of a mountain. Across the valley, on another mountain top, was the camp of the Philistines. When David reached King Saul's camp, he found all the soldiers gathered together, looking down into the valley. In the valley stood a man. He was tall as a giant and he carried a great, shining sword.

"I am Goliath, the Philistine giant," he cried. "Come down and fight, men of Israel!"

The soldiers of Israel trembled with fear.

"For shame!" cried David. "Maybe you are afraid to fight this giant, but I am not!"

"Go back to your sheep where you belong!" cried David's brothers.

But David would not go home.

"Take me to King Saul!" he said.

David begged the king to let him fight Goliath.

"Once I killed a lion that was attacking my sheep," David told Saul. "God was with me then. He will be with me now."

Saul told his men to bring David a sword and some armor, but David shook his head.

"I will take only my sling and some stones," he said.

"May God go with you!" said King Saul.

In a mountain brook, David found five stones that were smooth and round. Then he went to meet Goliath.

When the giant saw the young boy coming to fight him, he roared with laughter.

"You may laugh if you please," said David, "but you have only a sword. I have the help of God!"

Goliath rushed forward with an angry roar. Quick and sure, David drew back his sling and sent a stone flying through the air. It struck the giant's head like a bullet, and he fell to the ground. Then David took Goliath's own sword and cut off the giant's head. When the Philistine soldiers saw this, they all ran away like frightened rabbits.

Forward charged the mighty giant
Holding high his shining sword.
But David's small stone struck him down
For David had faith in the Lord.

Everyone in Israel sang the praises of David the shepherd boy, who had killed a giant and saved his people from the Philistines.

Jonathan Saves David

Everyone in Israel was talking about David, the brave soldier.

"This man is a great leader," the people said.

Now when King Saul heard what the people were saying, he became so jealous of David that he decided to kill him. But David found out about Saul's wicked plan, and it made him very sad, for David loved Saul dearly. He loved Jonathan, the king's son, even more. David and Jonathan had grown up together and cared for each other like brothers.

"I will tell Jonathan that Saul wants to kill me," thought David, "and perhaps he can help me."

But Jonathan would not believe that his father planned to do such a wicked thing.

"I must find out for myself if it is true!" he told David.

"But it is not safe for me to stay here," said David.

"Go into the fields and stay for three days," said Jonathan. "Then come back and hide in the pile of rocks just outside the city.

I will pretend I am going hunting, and I will come near the rocks with my quiver of arrows. I will bring a small boy with me. I will shoot three arrows to the side. If I have found out my father does not want to kill you, I will say: 'The arrows are in front of you.' But if you hear me say: 'The arrows are beyond you,' then you must flee for your life!"

David and Jonathan wept as they said goodbye.

"Promise me that if I die you will make sure my family is cared for," said Jonathan.

"Your family will never suffer while I live," David promised.

Then David went into the fields, and at the end of three days he came back and hid among the rocks. Soon he heard footsteps, a boy's and a man's. Then came the faint twang of a bowstring as three arrows were shot into the air. David's heart beat fast as he waited for Jonathan to speak. Then he heard his friend say:

"The arrows have gone beyond you, boy!"

When David heard these words, his heart was filled with sorrow, for now he knew without any doubt that Saul wanted to kill him.

Near the rocks where David was hiding,
Jonathan shot the arrows three.
"They've gone beyond": the king's son cried,
And David knew that he must flee.

As David left his hiding place, he heard Jonathan whisper:

"May God go with you, David. And remember, I am your friend forever!"

Then Jonathan went back to the city, and David began his long days of wandering in strange lands.

David Spares King Saul's Life

"**S**aul has slain his thousands,
And David his ten thousands."

This was the song all Israel was singing. When King Saul heard the people singing the praises of David, he became very jealous.

"Soon they will want David for their king," he thought. "I will send him away to battle and perhaps he will be killed."

But wherever David went, God watched over him and kept him safe from harm. But David's heart was sad, for he knew King Saul wanted him to die.

At last David could bear the king's hatred no longer. He fled to the mountains to hide in the caves. Many soldiers of Israel followed him there, for they knew David was a better leader than Saul.

King Saul was filled with rage when he found out that David had fled.

"I will find him and kill him if I have to search forever!" he cried.

With three thousand of his best soldiers, Saul went hunting for David. At the foot of a steep mountain, Saul told his men to halt.

"Go ahead without me and search every cave," he told them. "I will climb this mountain and search alone."

Up and up climbed Saul, until he came to a deep cave. Saul was very tired from his long climb. He stepped inside the cave, where it was dark and cool. Saul lay down on the floor of the cave and was soon fast asleep. Little did he dream that close by him in the darkness was the man he hunted. David and his men had chosen this very cave for their hiding place!

David and his men had seen the king come into the cave, but David had raised his fingers to his lips so his men would be silent. After Saul was asleep, one of David's men said:

"Now is your chance to kill him!"

"No!" said David. Then, walking on tiptoe, David went to the king's side. With his sword, he cut the skirt off the king's robe.

While King Saul slept like a tiny babe
In a mountain cave dark and deep,
David cut the skirt off his robe
Without even waking the king from his sleep!

When Saul awoke from his nap, he yawned and stretched and walked out of the cave into the bright sunlight. But as he started down the mountain, he heard a voice call out.

"My lord, the king!"

Saul looked behind him, and there stood David, holding in his hand the skirt from Saul's robe. Saul could hardly believe his eyes.

"You could have killed me," he said, "why didn't you?"

David knelt before the king.

"I could not," he said, "for that is not the way of the Lord."

Saul bowed his head and wept.

"You are a good man, David," he said, "but I am a sinful one. Now I am sure you will soon be king of Israel."

David, King of Israel

Saul, King of Israel, was dead! He had lost a great battle against the Philistines. Saul fell upon his own sword and died bravely, so that the enemy could not take him prisoner. Jonathan, son of King Saul, was killed in this same terrible battle.

When David heard the news that these two great men had died, he wept for many days. Even though Saul had tried to kill him, David loved the king, and Jonathan had been his best friend.

But now Jonathan and Saul were dead, and Israel was without a leader.

The tribes of the north thought that Ishbosheth, son of Saul, should be king; but the southern tribes wanted David. And so Israel was divided. The people of the north chose Ishbosheth. The people of the south chose David.

But the people of the north soon grew tired of Ishbosheth, for he was a very weak king. One night, as he lay asleep, some men crept into his tent and killed him. The people of the north thought David would be pleased to hear this news, but instead, David was very angry.

"These men will be punished for their wicked deed!" he cried.

Then the leaders of the northern tribes said:

"David is a just man. Let us ask him to be our king."

And so David became king of all Israel, and once more the tribes were united as one nation.

King Saul fought a mighty battle
And died upon his sword.
Then Israel chose to be their king,
David, who loved the Lord.

David chose the city of Jerusalem for the capital of Israel. But at that time, Jerusalem was held by Israeli's enemies, the Jebusites.

"Our army must capture Jerusalem," said David. "With the help of God it will be ours!"

But the Jebusites laughed when they heard that the army of Israel was coming to capture Jerusalem. They put all their blind and crippled people on the walls of the city.

"They think we are so weak that even the lame and the blind could turn us back," said David.

But the Jebusites soon found out that they were wrong. The soldiers of Israel fought hard and well; Jerusalem was soon captured and became the capital of Israel.

To Jerusalem came masons and carpenters, sent by King Hiram of Tyre to help build a palace for David, the King.

The palace was made of fragrant cedar wood and when it was finished, David stood on the rooftop, looking out over Jerusalem. He looked up at the bright blue sky and asked God to help him be a good king.

David and Mephibosheth

Under the rule of King David, Israel became a rich and mighty nation. The kings of other nations came to Jerusalem to honor King David, for they had heard of his great courage and wisdom.

But even though David had become rich and famous, he did not forget his old friends.

One day, David stood on the rooftop of his palace, looking out over the city. From a courtyard below, he could hear the laughter of children. David thought of the days when he had been a boy in Bethlehem. Then he thought of Jonathan, son of King Saul, who had been his dearest friend. Jonathan had died beside King Saul in battle. But as in a dream, David seemed to hear Jonathan say:

"Promise me, David, that if I die, you will always care for my family."

David called his servant to him and said:

"Can you tell me if anyone in Saul's family is still alive?"

"I do not know," said the servant, "but Ziba could tell you. He was once King Saul's servant."

"Send for him at once," said David.

When Ziba stood before him, David said:

"Are there any members of Saul's family still alive?"

"There is Mephibosheth," said the old man. "He is Jonathan's son."

"Bring the boy here to the palace!" cried David.

The next day, as King David sat on his throne, he saw coming towards him, led by a servant, a thin, pale boy with sad dark eyes. As the boy walked, he dragged one leg behind him and his thin body shook with fright.

When the boy reached the throne, he fell to his knees before the king. He hid his face in his arms and cried:

"Why did you want to see a poor cripple like me. I am no better than a dead dog!"

The great king stepped down from his thone. Kneeling beside the boy, he lifted him gently to his feet.

"Who are you?" he asked.

"I am Mephibosheth," said the boy.

"You are Jonathan's son," said King David.

The heart of the little lame boy was suddenly filled with joy. For in the voice of the king, he heard great kindness, and in the king's eyes he saw great love.

From that day on, Mephibosheth ate his meals at the king's table like the king's own son. David gave him all the land that had once belonged to Saul. Thus did David prove that he was not only a very great king, but a very kind man as well.

To the palace of the great King David
Came Jonathan's son, thin and lame.
And the great king proved that love and
*   kindness*
Meant more to him than wealth or fame.

Solomon Is Chosen King

All Israel was filled with sadness. People stood before the gates of the great palace in Jerusalem, weeping and praying. For inside the palace, the beloved King David lay dying.

But there was one man in Jerusalem who was not sad. He was Adonijah, King David's oldest son. Even though his father lay on his deathbed, Adonijah rode through the streets in a fine chariot, guarded by soldiers, and shouted:

"Make way for your new king!"

Then Adonijah decided to celebrate with a great feast. He invited Joab, the general of King David's army, and Abiathar, the priest.

Then Nathan, the great prophet, heard the news that Adonijah was boasting of becoming king. Nathan went to Bath-sheba, wife of King David, and said:

"Did you know that Adonijah is planning to be king? At this very moment he sits at a great feast and the men around him cry: 'Long live the king!'"

"But King David promised me that my son Solomon would be king," cried Bath-sheba. Then she hurried to David's bedside.

The great king lay with his eyes closed. The lips that had once sung such joyous songs were now still and pale.

"My Lord," said Bath-sheba. Slowly, the king opened his eyes.

"You once promised me that Solomon would be Israel's next king," Bath-sheba said. "Now Adonijah claims that right. I am afraid if he becomes king he will kill both Solomon and me. You must speak now and say who is to take your place!"

"Tell Nathan to come in," said David.

When the prophet stood at his bedside, David said:

"Tell the high priest Zadok to anoint Solomon king this very day."

A few hours later, Solomon was anointed king of Israel. When Adonijah heard this news, he was very frightened.

"Solomon will order my death!" he cried. But Solomon said:

"If Adonijah obeys the laws, no harm will ever come to him."

All Israel waited and wondered,
"Who will be king when David dies?"
"I will be king!" boasted Adonijah,
But David chose Solomon, strong and wise.

Soon after Solomon was anointed, King David died. There was great sorrow and weeping in Israel, for David had been dearly loved by all his people. Under his wise rule, Israel had become a great nation.

Hundreds of years have passed since that long-ago time, but the world still sings the songs of David, the shepherd boy who became a king.

God's Beautiful House

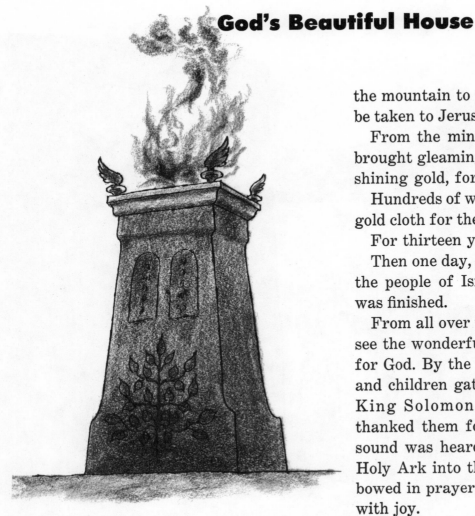

"I am going to build the most beautiful house in all the world for God!"

These were the words of the great King Solomon of Israel.

"I shall build God's temple of fragrant cedar," he said, "and the door knobs and hinges will be made of pure gold."

Solomon sent for King Hiram of Tyre to come to Jerusalem.

"I want you to send me cedar trees from Lebanon," Solomon told King Hiram, "so that I may build a temple for the Lord. For this, I will send you each year many bushels of wheat and many gallons of olive oil."

King Hiram ordered his men to cut down hundreds of trees in the cedar forests of Lebanon. Then the trees were hauled from the mountain to the sea and put on rafts to be taken to Jerusalem.

From the mines, deep in the earth, men brought gleaming copper, bright silver, and shining gold, for God's great temple.

Hundreds of women sewed on fine silk and gold cloth for the House of the Lord.

For thirteen years, the work went on.

Then one day, King Solomon sent word to the people of Israel that the great temple was finished.

From all over the land the people came to see the wonderful house the king had built for God. By the hundreds the men, women, and children gathered at the great temple. King Solomon stood before them and thanked them for their hard work. Not a sound was heard as the priest carried the Holy Ark into the temple. Every head was bowed in prayer, and every heart was filled with joy.

Inside the temple, the red wood of the cedars of Lebanon gleamed in the light of many candles. He had made an altar of gold. On each side of the altar were five beautiful golden candlesticks. The silken hangings of the Holy of Holies were all the colors of the rainbow.

Truly, Solomon had built for God the most beautiful house in all the world!

From the cedar forests of Lebanon
Many hundreds of miles away
Came the fragrant wood for the house of God
Where Israel could worship and pray.
On each side of the altar stood
Five candlesticks of purest gold.
The House King Solomon built for God
Was wondrous to behold!

The Wisdom of Solomon

High in the mountains at a place called Gibeon Solomon, the new king of Israel, came to pray. As he prayed, he heard the voice of God say:

"What shall I give you, Solomon? Ask, and it shall be yours."

"Oh, Lord," said Solomon, "give me an understanding heart, so that I may rule my people with wisdom."

"I will give you what you ask," said God, "and even though you did not ask for great wealth, I will give you that also."

As the years passed, Solomon became very rich, and his judgment was so wise that even people in far-off lands spoke with wonder of his wisdom.

One day, as Solomon sat on his great throne, a servant came to him and said:

"Sire, two women wait outside to see you. One carries an infant and each woman claims the child as hers."

"Send them in," ordered the king.

The servant led the two women to the throne. One woman held a baby close to her breast. The other woman was weeping.

"What brings you here to the palace?" asked Solomon. Both women began talking at once.

"This child is mine!" cried the woman who held the baby.

"He belongs to me!" cried the other woman.

"Silence!" commanded the king. "Give the child to me."

The woman put the infant into the arms of the king, and Solomon smiled kindly down at the small rosy face. Then he said:

"Tell me your story, one at a time."

"Sire," said the woman who had been weeping, "this woman and I live in the same house. Each of us had a baby son. But last night, this woman's son died. Creeping into my room while I slept, she took my own living son from his cradle and put her dead son in his place."

"She lies!"cried the other woman. "It was her son who died!" King Solomon turned to a servant and said:

"Bring me a sharp sword."

When the servant had brought the sword, the king said:

"Cut this child in half so that each woman will have a part of him."

The woman who had brought in the baby looked very pleased.

But the other woman flung herself at Solomon's feet.

"No, no!" she screamed. "Give the child to the other woman, but please do not kill him!"

Solomon raised the woman gently to her feet. He put the baby into her arms and said:

"You are the real mother, for you thought only of what was best for the child."

Two women brought a child to Solomon's throne
Each one claiming the child as her own.
"Bring me a sword," wise Solomon cried,
"This child in half I will divide!"

Elijah, The Prophet

When wise King Solomon died, there was no great leader to take his place. The tribes of Israel became divided, into two kingdoms; Judah in the south, Israel in the north.

The years passed, and there came to the throne of Israel a king named Ahab, who had a wicked wife named Jezebel. Jezebel ordered many temples built throughout the land for the false god, Baal.

Now in the tribe of Gilead there was a good and wise man called Elijah. Elijah walked from village to village, speaking the word of God to the people. But as Elijah traveled through the land, his heart became very sad, for everywhere he went, he saw people starving. There had been very little rain in the land and the grain had withered in the fields. But King Ahab and his wicked wife Jezebel feasted on plenty in their fine palace and did not care what happened to the people.

One day, as King Ahab was riding through the country, a man jumped out of the bushes at the side of the road. The man's clothes were covered with dust and his eyes blazed with anger.

"Halt!" cried the man.

The king saw that the man was Elijah, the prophet. Elijah pointed his finger at the king and cried:

"There will not be any rain in the land for many years!"

Then Elijah ran away as fast as he could. On and on he ran, until he came to the gate of a city. Outside the city walls he saw a woman was gathering sticks.

"I beg of you," said Elijah to the woman, "bring me water and food."

The woman brought Elijah a cup of water and said:

"I am a poor widow. My son is very ill and I have just enough meal and oil in my house to bake one more loaf of bread."

"Bake your bread and do not fear," said Elijah. "God will send you more meal and oil."

The woman went into her house and baked the bread. Lo and behold! Each time she emptied the jars of meal and oil they became full again.

"You must not fear to bake your bread,"
Elijah to the widow said.
"Use all the meal and oil, and then,
God will fill the jars again."

But even though the woman's son had plenty to eat, he died.

"My son has died," the woman wept. "You came to kill him."

And Elijah said to her, "Clean the house well and boil all the drinking water, I will care for your son."

Elijah then fell to his knees beside the dead boy's bed and cried:

"Oh, Lord, let this boy live!"

God answered Elijah's prayer, for the boy came back to life.

The widow threw herself at Elijah's feet. Tears of joy filled her eyes.

"You are indeed a man of God," she said.

When the people in the village heard how Elijah had brought back to life the widow's son, they destroyed the altars of Baal and began to worship the one true God, the God of Israel.

Elijah and the Prophets of Baal

There had been much suffering in the land of Israel. No rain had fallen for many months and the grain had withered in the fields. Mothers wept as they listened to their children crying for bread.

At that time, Israel was ruled by King Ahab and the wicked Queen Jezebel, who worshiped the false god, Baal. Many of the people also worshiped this false god.

But there was one man who loved the Lord with all his heart. This man was Elijah, the prophet. Elijah went from village to village, speaking the word of God and trying to cheer the people.

One night, God spoke to Elijah and said:

"Go before King Ahab and then I will send rain."

Elijah obeyed the Lord's command and when he stood before Ahab, the king said:

"Have you come here to cause more trouble?"

"It is you who have caused trouble," said Elijah, "for you have made the people worship false gods."

"Why doesn't your God send rain?" said the king.

"Tell the people and the four-hundred-and-fifty prophets of Baal to come to Mount Carmel," said Elijah. "You will see why God does not send rain!"

"Very well," said Ahab.

When all the people had gathered on Mount Carmel, Elijah cried out:

"Let the prophets of Baal place a bullock and some wood on the altar and call upon their god to set the wood afire!"

The prophets of Baal made ready their sacrifice. Then they began to chant:

"Oh, mighty Baal, set the wood afire."

All that day, the prophets prayed and wept and cried out to Baal. But the wood did not burn.

Then Elijah built an altar with twelve stones, and dug a trench around it. Upon the altar he laid some wood and a bullock. Then he said to the people:

"Pour water over this offering."

Three times the people poured water over the wood and the bullock until the trench was filled. Then Elijah fell to his knees and cried:

"Oh, Lord, show the people you are the one true God of Israel!"

Every pair of eyes was turned towards the altar.

Suddenly, there came a loud, crackling noise, and a burst of flame. The wood began to burn, and the water in the trench was soon dried up.

The people fell to their knees.

"The Lord He is God!" they cried.

Late that night, the rain began to pour down from the heavens.

There was no more famine in the land, for the people now worshiped the Lord, the true God of Israel.

From every tribe of Israel
To Mount Carmel the people came.
They gazed in wonder when they saw
Elijah's wood burst into flame!

Elijah and the Ravens

In the lonely hill country, Elijah the great prophet sat quietly beside a bubbling brook. As the clear water went dancing over the stones, it seemed to say to Elijah:

"Come, be happy, for the sun is bright and the world is a beautiful place!"

The birds in the trees sang to Elijah and seemed to say:

"Come, sing with us and be merry, for the sky is blue and the world is full of joy."

But Elijah did not hear the laughter of the brook or the singing of the birds, for his heart was heavy with sadness. There had been no rain in the land for many months, and the people were starving. But King Ahab and his wicked wife, Jezebel, had plenty to eat and cared nothing for the people. The king had built many temples to Baal, and the people worshiped the ugly idols of this false god. Elijah went before the king and told him there would be no rain for a long time. This made King Ahab very angry. Then God spoke to Elijah and said:

"Go into the hills beside the brook and hide from the king. The brook will give you water to drink, and I will send ravens to bring your food."

Elijah had been sitting beside the brook for a long time, and he was very hungry. Suddenly, he heard a great flapping of wings. He looked above him and saw a large flock of big, black birds. Elijah gazed in wonder as the birds flew lower and lower. Then, suddenly, through the air, bread and meat came falling. The ravens had brought Elijah the food God had promised!

Through the air the ravens came
Bringing bread and meat.
Flying o'er Elijah's head,
They dropped food at his feet.

After Elijah had eaten the food, he drank cool, clear water from the brook. Every morning and every evening, the ravens brought food to the prophet. And every morning and every evening, Elijah thanked God for taking such good care of him.

Elisha and the Loaves of Bread

The great teacher, Elisha, had come to Gilgal to speak the word of God to some young men who were learning to be prophets. But the young men were very troubled, for their grain had not grown well that year and they had no food to offer Elisha. Not far away, in another city, there lived a man who was a very dear friend of Elisha. When this man heard that the great teacher had come to Gilgal to see the young men, he said to himself:

"I will go to see my dear friend and take him a gift."

The man put twenty loaves of bread and some ears of corn into a bag. Then he set out on his journey to Gilgal.

Elisha was very happy to see his friend and thanked him for the bag of food.

"Put the loaves of bread and the ears of corn upon the table," Elisha told his servant. "Then call the young men and tell them to come and eat."

"But sir, there are only twenty loaves of bread," said the servant, "and there are a hundred young men!"

"God has told me there will be enough food for everyone," said Elisha, "There will even be some left. Do as I tell you and put the food upon the table."

The servant put the loaves of bread and the ears of corn on the table. Then he called to the young men.

When the young men saw the fresh loaves of bread, with delicious, golden-brown crusts, they sat right down at the table and began to eat as fast as they could. But even though there were a hundred young men and only twenty loaves of bread, there was plenty for everyone. When the young men had finished eating they gazed at the table in wonder, for there was still some food left. Then they bowed their heads and thanked God for taking such good care of them.

A hundred men had to be fed,
And of loaves there were just twenty.
"Trust in the Lord," Elisha said.
"For He promised there'd be plenty!"

The Story of Naaman

In the country of Aram there lived a very rich man called Naaman. Naaman was the general of all the armies. But all of Naaman's riches could not make him happy, for he had the terrible disease, leprosy. Day after day, Naaman sat in his fine house, speaking to no one, not even his beautiful wife.

One day, as Naaman's wife sat weeping, a young slave girl came to her and said:

"Please do not weep, my lady, for I think I can help you."

Naaman's wife looked at the girl in surprise.

"I was brought here as a captive from Israel," said the girl, "and in my country there lives a great prophet called Elisha. He can cure your husband."

Naaman's wife ran to her husband to tell him what the slave girl had said. Then Naaman went to the king of Aram and told him about the great prophet Elisha. The king wrote a letter, and said to Naaman:

"Take this letter to the king of Israel."

Riding in a fine chariot, Naaman began his journey to Israel. With him he took ten changes of clothing, and talents of silver.

The king of Israel was greatly honored that Naaman, the great general, had come to visit him. But when Naaman gave him the letter from the king of Aram, these were the words the king of Israel read:

"Namaan, my servant, comes to you to be cured of leprosy."

"I know of no cure for leprosy," cried the king. His heart was filled with dread, for he greatly feared the powerful ruler of Aram.

But Elisha, the prophet, soon heard about Naaman's visit. Elisha went to the king of Israel and said:

"Send Naaman to me."

But when Naaman came to Elisha's house, the prophet sent a messenger out to meet him.

"You must bathe seven times in the River Jordan and then you will be cured," said the messenger. "These are the words of the prophet!"

"I could have bathed in the rivers of Damascus in my own land!" cried Naaman, and he drove away in a great rage. But his servants ran after him crying:

"Wait, master! It will do no harm to try!"

Naaman pulled his horses to a stop.

"You are right!" he said.

Lo and behold! After Naaman had bathed seven times in the Jordan, his leprosy was cured! He went back to Elisha's house and offered the prophet gifts of silver and fine clothing. But Elisha said:

"I will take nothing. Go in peace."

Then Naaman, the great general, fell to his knees before Elisha and cried:

"Mighty and wondrous are the powers of the God of Israel!"

Namaan bathed in the Jordan
And when he came back to the shore
Lo and behold! His hands were clean.
He had the dread disease no more!

How Jeremiah Was Saved

Long ago, in Jerusalem, there lived a very great and good man named Jeremiah. One day, God spoke to Jeremiah and told him to warn the people of the land of Benjamin that they must flee, for the army of the king of Babylon would soon take them captives.

Jeremiah left Jerusalem and journeyed to the land of Benjamin to obey God's command. When he told the people what was going to happen, they became very frightened.

Now the princes of the land were very angry when they heard what Jeremiah was saying to the people. They seized him and threw him into a deep, dark dungeon. Then they went to the king and said:

"You must order this man Jeremiah put to death. He goes about the city trying to frighten the people by warning them of great trouble that is coming."

But one of the king's officers was a very kind and good man named Ebed-melech the Ethiopian. Ebed-melech went to the king and said:

"Jeremiah is a great prophet. He is only trying to help us. I beg you to take him from the dungeon or he will starve. He has had no food for days."

The king believed what Ebed-melech had told him and said:

"Take thirty men and lift Jeremiah from the dungeon."

The dungeon into which Jeremiah had been thrown was so deep that the men had to lift him out with long ropes. But how happy Jeremiah was when he stood in the sunlight once more, with the damp, cold air of the dungeon no longer chilling him through and through. He knelt in prayer to thank God for sending a kind man like Ebed-melech the kindly Ethiopian to help him.

Down in a cold, dreary dungeon
Jeremiah the prophet lay.
The dungeon was so dark and deep,
He could not see the light of day.

The Lost Book

Long ago, there was a very good king who ruled over the people of Judah. His name was Josiah, and he loved and trusted God and prayed to Him each day.

But King Josiah was very troubled because the Temple of God had become very shabby. Many of the kings who ruled before Josiah had worshiped idols and had not kept the Temple in good condition. Under the rule of these kings, the people had forgotten about God and never visited His beautiful house to pray.

King Josiah decided to make God's Temple beautiful and shining once more. He ordered his workmen to repair and clean the Temple and make it like new.

The workmen cleaned and swept and scrubbed. All the beautiful colors in the Temple that had become dull with dust and dirt seemed to come to life again. The brass and copper ornaments and the gold candlesticks were scoured and polished until they sparkled and gleamed.

Then one day, while the work was going on, a wonderful thing happened. Under a thick pile of dust, one of the priests found a book. When he opened it, he saw that it was a book of God's holy laws. The priest took the book to a wise man called Shaphan, who was a very good reader. Shaphan read the book and then he took it to King Josiah.

"This is a very precious book," said Shaphan, "for in it are written the holy laws which God gave to Moses."

"Read me every word in the book," said the king.

After the king had heard every word in the book, he called all the people together. He told them about all the holy laws in this wonderful book. Then he promised the people that he would always obey these laws. The people promised the king that they, too, would obey the laws which had been given to their fathers so many years ago.

There was great feasting and celebrating all through the land because the lost book of holy laws had been found.

God's house had grown very shabby
It was covered with dirt and with rust.
But a book of holy laws was found
Lying buried deep in the dust.

Jonah and the Whale

In the village of Galilee, there lived a man called Jonah. One night, Jonah heard the voice of God say:

"Arise, and go to the city of Nineveh! Tell the people I will destroy their city unless they stop their evil ways."

But Jonah was afraid to go to Nineveh, so he ran away. He went to a city by the sea and got on a ship that was ready to sail for Tarshish. Soon after the ship set sail, a terrible storm sprang up. Giant waves rocked the ship back and forth like a toy cradle. The wind howled like an angry old witch. But Jonah heard not a sound, for he had fallen fast asleep in the deepest part of the ship. The other people on the ship prayed that the storm would stop, but instead it grew worse.

"Someone on the ship is causing this storm!" cried the people. "Let us draw lots and see who it is!"

The captain of the ship went to awaken Jonah, and shouted:

"Come! Cast your lot with the others! Perhaps it is you who is causing the storm?"

When the lots were cast, the lot fell to Jonah.

"God is angry with me because I did not obey Him," Jonah told the people. "You must throw me into the sea or you will all be drowned."

As soon as the people had thrown Jonah overboard, the sea became calm.

Down, down, down went Jonah, into the angry waters. Then suddenly, he felt warm and safe. He opened his eyes and looked around him with wonder. He had been swallowed by a great whale and was now safe and sound in the whale's belly. For three days, Jonah lived inside the whale. Then suddenly, the whale spat Jonah out and he landed KERPLUNK! on dry land. Then God spoke to him again and said:

"Go to Nineveh and obey my command!"

All day and all night Jonah walked until he reached Nineveh. He ran through the streets of the city crying:

"In forty days, Nineveh will be destroyed!"

When the people heard these words, they became frightened and asked God to forgive them. When God saw how sorry the people were, he decided not to destroy the city.

Now Jonah was waiting outside Nineveh to see the city destroyed. He waited and waited, but nothing happened at all. Night came and he shivered in the cold wind. Then he saw a strange sight. All around him a big gourd was growing. It grew and grew until it made a warm, cozy little house and Jonah soon fell fast asleep. But in the morning, when he awoke, a large worm was eating up the gourd. When the gourd was gone, a hot wind sprang up and Jonah thought he would die from the terrible heat.

Then God spoke to him once more.

"Are you sorry the gourd is gone, Jonah?" asked God.

"Yes," said Jonah, "I felt sad when it was destroyed."

"Then you know how I feel about destroying a whole city full of people," said God.

Jonah stood in silence, thinking of how wonderful and true was the love God had for all His children.

Jonah lived inside a whale
And then inside a gourd.
Everywhere that Jonah went,
He was cared for by the Lord.

The Fiery Furnace

Long ago, in Babylon, there lived a king called Nebuchadnezzar. King Nebuchadnezzar built a huge golden idol and sent word to all the great men in his kingdom to gather before it. Before the ugly golden image, on a golden throne, sat the king. When all the satraps and judges and rulers had arrived, the king cried:

"When you hear the music of the lyres and trumpets, you must bow down to the golden image. Any man who does not will be thrown into a fiery furnace and will be burned to death!"

The music began, and all the great men bowed down before the idol. But there were three men who would not bow down before it. Some of the people went to the king and told him about the three men who had not obeyed his command.

"Bring the men to me!" cried the king to his soldiers.

"Who are you?" asked the king when the three men stood before him.

"I am Shadrach," said the first man.

"I am Meshach," said the second.

"I am Abed-nego," said the third. "We worship only one God and He is the Lord."

"If you do not bow down to the idol," said the king, "I will have you thrown into the fiery furnace!"

"We are not afraid," said the men, "for God will save us."

King Nebuchadnezzar shook with rage.

"Build the fire up seven times hotter," he cried to his soldiers, "and cast these men into the flames."

The soldiers bound Shadrach, Meshach and Abed-nego with ropes and threw them into the roaring fire. The fire was so hot that great flames leaped out from the furnace and burned some of the soldiers to death.

But lo and behold! When King Nebuchadnezzar came to look into the furnace at the three men, he saw a strange and wondrous sight.

Shadrach, Meshach and Abed-nego were walking about inside the furnace with the flames leaping up around them but not burning them one bit. And with them walked an Angel of God, sent to protect them from the terrible fire. Nebuchadnezzar fell to his knees and cried out:

"Shadrach, Meshach and Abed-nego! Come out of the fiery furnace!"

When the three men walked out of the fire, not a hair of their heads was harmed. Their clothes were not even scorched.

"Go in peace," the king told them, "for God has saved you with His mighty power."

King Nebuchadnezzar ordered all the people of Babylon to honor the God of Israel. Shadrach, Meshach and Abed-nego were given high positions in Babylon.

Inside the great fiery furnace
Among the flames roaring and hot
The three men walked with an Angel
And the blazing fire burned them not.

The Handwriting on the Wall

King Belshazzar was having a great feast in his palace, for he had just won a great battle with the Medes and the Persians. The palace was filled with many great treasures stolen from the people of other lands. Among these treasures were the gold and silver cups which the king's father, Nebuchadnezzar, had taken from the Temple at Jerusalem.

Now as King Belshazzar sat at the feast table with all his lords around him, he cried:

"Let us fill the cups from the Temple of Jerusalem with wine and drink a toast to our many victories!"

When the cups were filled, the king rose to his feet. He lifted his cup high, and cried:

"I drink to the gods of iron, brass, wood and stone!"

A great shout went up from the people, and every cup was raised.

Then, suddenly, a shadow seemed to fall across the room, and the king's face turned white as chalk. With a shaking finger, he pointed to the wall. The people turned to look and then screamed with fright. For across the wall was moving the shadow of a giant hand. Suddenly, the hand was gone, but upon the wall these words were written:

"Mene, mene, tekel upharsin!"

"What strange words are these?" everyone cried.

The king called in all the wise men in the land, but not one of them could tell him what the strange words meant. Then the Queen spoke.

"There is a man called Daniel," she said, "who was brought here as a captive from Judah. He is very wise and may be able to tell you the meaning of these words."

"Send for him at once!" cried the king.

When Daniel stood before him, King Belshazzar said:

"If you can tell me the meaning of those words upon the wall, I will make you a ruler in my kingdom."

"I care nothing for gifts," said Daniel, "but I can tell you what the words mean. They mean that the days of your kingdom are numbered. You will be punished, just as God punished your dead father King Nebuchadnezzar. Your kingdom will be divided between the Medes and the Persians."

The king groaned with fear. Then he commanded his servants to dress Daniel in purple robes and put a gold chain around his neck. Daniel was made one of the highest rulers in the kingdom.

But that very night, spies of the Medes and Persians crept into the palace and murdered King Belshazzar while he slept. His kingdom was divided between the Medes and the Persians.

The handwriting on the wall had told the truth.

While King Belshazzar sat feasting,
Upon the wall a hand did write
Strange words no one could understand
That made the great king shake with fright.

Daniel in the Lions' Den

After the death of King Belshazzar, Darius the Mede ruled over Babylon. King Darius chose three presidents to rule under him, and one of these presidents was Daniel, of Judah. Daniel was a wise and just ruler and was dearly loved by the king and by all the people. But the other rulers were very jealous of Daniel and made a wicked plan to destroy him.

These jealous rulers knew that Daniel prayed to the God of Israel three times each day. So one day, they went to King Darius and said:

"Oh, great king, we have decided you should make a new law which says that in the next thirty days, nobody may ask a favor of any god or man but only of you. If any man disobeys this law, he shall be thrown into a den of lions! This law will keep peace in the land."

"If such a law will help keep peace, then write it down and I will sign it," said the king.

Now in those long-ago times, if a law was signed by the king, it could never be changed. After Darius had signed the new law the jealous rulers went to spy upon Daniel. They found him kneeling in prayer, facing towards Jerusalem.

"Daniel, the law says you must not ask favors of anyone except the king!" cried the rulers.

"I do no wrong," said Daniel, "and I shall always worship the God of Israel, for His laws are greater than any laws made by a king!"

Then the jealous rulers went to the king and said:

"Every day, Daniel breaks your law, for he kneels and asks favors of his God. You must throw him to the lions!"

When the king heard this, he was sorry he had signed the new law, for he did not want to see Daniel killed. But he knew the law could not be changed. With a heavy heart, he ordered his soldiers to sieze Daniel and throw him into the lions' den.

After the soldiers had thrown Daniel into the den of roaring lions, they rolled a huge stone against the opening so that he could not escape.

All that night, King Darius lay awake in his palace, thinking of Daniel being clawed and torn to bits by the hungry beasts. As soon as morning came, the king hurried to the lions' den. He was afraid to call out to Daniel for he feared he was dead. Finally, in a trembling voice, Darius cried out:

"Daniel, has your God saved you from the lions?"

Then the king's heart filled with joy, for Daniel's voice answered him, strong and clear:

"Yes, oh king, an Angel of God came and shut the lions' mouths so they could not hurt me!"

"Has God saved you from the lions?"
Outside Darius cried.

"Yes, oh king!" Daniel answered him.
"For an Angel walked by my side!"

The king commanded his soldiers to roll the stone away from the opening of the den and Daniel walked out unharmed, with not a single scratch upon his body.

King Darius punished the jealous rulers and made a new law that said everyone in the kingdom should worship the God of Israel.

The King Who Gave Gifts to God

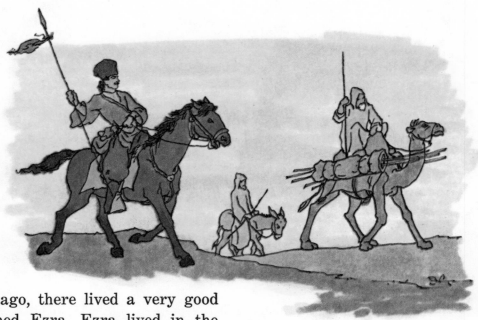

Long, long ago, there lived a very good man named Ezra. Ezra lived in the great kingdom ruled by King Artaxerxes. One day, Ezra decided to go to Jerusalem to see if the people there were obeying the laws of God. But he knew that he could not go unless he asked the king.

When he went before the king, he was very surprised and pleased, for the king said:

"Yes, Ezra, I will allow you to go to Jerusalem as soon as you wish. And anyone else from this kingdom who wishes to go with you will also be allowed to do so."

Ezra was filled with great joy and he thanked the king for being so kind. Then he turned to leave, but King Artaxerxes cried:

"Wait! That is not all. I know that the people of Jerusalem are building a temple for the God of Israel. I shall give you some precious vessels to take there as my gifts for the Temple. I will give you money, also, so that you may buy anything you need for the House of God."

"Go, Ezra, and take my gifts,"
  Said the great and mighty king.
"To the Temple of your God,
  "Precious jars and vessels bring."

Imagine how happy Ezra was when he heard these words! He told all his friends what the king had said, and many of them decided to make the journey with him.

Before Ezra left for Jerusalem, the king gave him a letter.

"Show this letter to the rulers in all the countries you travel through," said the king, "and they will give you wheat and oil and other precious gifts."

Ezra fell to his knees and cried:

"Blessed be the Lord God of our fathers, for He has touched the king's heart with much kindness!"

King Artaxerxes proved that he had an unselfish heart and wanted to share his great riches with others.

Nehemiah Builds a Wall

In the palace of the great King Artaxerxes, there was an attendant called Nehemiah. One day, the king noticed that Nehemiah looked very sad.

"What is troubling you, Nehemiah?" asked the king. "For many days you have seemed very unhappy."

"Oh, King," cried Nehemiah, "I have reason to be sad. In Jerusalem, the city of my birth, the great wall has been destroyed, and the gates of the city burned to the ground."

"I am sorry to hear this," said the king. "Is there anything I can do to help you?"

"Oh, yes," cried Nehemiah, "allow me to go to Jerusalem, so that I may help the people build a new wall!"

"You may go as soon as you wish," said the king.

Nehemiah was filled with joy. He thanked the king and started on his journey.

When he reached Jerusalem, he rode all around the city on a little donkey. But with each step the donkey took, Nehemiah's heart became heavier and heavier. Alas! Where once had stood the great wall of Jerusalem, now was nothing but broken bricks and stones and pieces of burned wood. Nehemiah's eyes filled with tears as he looked at the ruins. But he knew that tears would not build a new wall, so he called all the people of Jerusalem together and said:

"We must build a new wall to protect our city against wild animals, and cruel enemies. If every man, woman and child will help, we can soon have the new wall finished. Come, let us begin the work at once!"

Not one person refused to help, and for many months, the people of Jerusalem were busy as bees. Then, at last, the wall was finished. The people were very proud of the wall they had all helped to build around their great city, and Nehemiah's heart was filled with gladness.

God was pleased, too, for He loves to see all His children working together.

Nehemiah cried, "Come one, come all!
"Around Jerusalem build a wall!"
The work was done by everyone
And soon the great new wall was done!

Queen Esther Saves Her People

Long ago, there lived a powerful king called Ahasuerus. In his great kingdom lived thousands of Jews who had been brought as captives from Judah. Among them was a young woman so sweet and beautiful that Ahasuerus chose her for his queen. Her name was Esther.

Before Esther became queen, she lived with her cousin, Mordecai, for her mother and father were dead. After Esther was chosen queen, Mordecai became a gatekeeper at the king's palace. One day, Mordecai heard two of the other gatekeepers planning to kill the king. Mordecai told Esther to warn the king about this wicked plan. The gatekeepers were punished and it was written in the Book of Chronicles that Mordecai had saved the king's life.

Now one of the king's advisors was a wicked man called Prince Haman. One day, Haman rode through the palace gates. All the gatekeepers except Mordecai bowed down to him. Haman was so angry that he swore he would kill Mordecai and every Jew in the land. He went to the king and said:

"There are people in your kingdom who do not keep your laws. Allow me to kill them and I will pay you ten thousand talents of silver."

"Do as you wish," said the king.

Haman ordered that all Jews be killed on the thirteenth day of the twelfth month. When Mordecai heard this terrible news, he sent word to Queen Esther that she must go to the king and ask him to spare her people.

Esther trembled as she entered the king's inner court, for nobody was allowed to go there unless asked by the king himself. Esther knew that if the king did not hold out his golden scepter to her, she would be put to death. But Ahasuerus smiled at her and held out the golden scepter.

"What do you wish?" he asked kindly.

"I wish to invite you and Prince Haman to dine with me tomorrow evening," said Queen Esther.

That evening, Prince Haman went to the palace to dine with Queen Esther and the king. After the meal was over, the king smiled at Esther and said:

"Do you wish a favor, my love?"

"Oh, sire," said Esther, her lovely eyes filled with tears, "I ask you to spare my people, for it has been ordered that they all be put to death!"

Then Esther pointed to Prince Haman and cried:

"And there sits the wicked man who gave the orders!"

Just then, a servant ran into the room and said to the king!

"Look outside at the gallows where Haman plans to hang Mordecai!"

When King Ahasuerus saw the gallows, he cried with anger:

"Let Haman hang there instead!"

Great was the joy of the Jews when they heard that Queen Esther had saved their lives. Now, hundreds of years later, at the holiday of Purim, all the Jews of the world celebrate the happy time when brave Queen Esther saved her people.

"Oh, spare my people, sire, I pray,"
  Cried brave Queen Esther to the king.
"Let them live!" the king commanded,
"And Haman to the gallows bring!"

Bravo Baryshnikov!

Bravo Baryshnikov!

Alan LeMond

With photographs by Lois Greenfield and others

Grosset & Dunlap
A Filmways Company
Publishers   New York

The publisher gratefully acknowledges permission to use the following:

"The Key." From *Modern Russian Poetry,* edited by Vladimir Markov and Merrill Sparks. Copyright © 1966, 1967 by MacGibbon & Kee, Ltd. Reprinted by permission of the Bobbs-Merrill Company, Inc.

Designed by Marcia Gloster Ben-Eli

First printing 1978
Printed in the United States of America

Contents

Le Grand Jeté West

I n the crisp early-morning hours of June 30, 1974, just outside the stage doors of Toronto's O'Keefe Centre, perhaps the most brilliant classical dancer the Soviet Union has ever produced executed the great leap to the West. Mikhail Baryshnikov defected.

It was one of his greatest performances. Certainly it was his most successful. Choreographed brilliantly, executed flawlessly, typically daring — Mikhail Baryshnikov's Canadian premiere of *"Le Grand Jeté West"* stunned the ballet world.

His astounding solo, performed only once, contained elements of suspense and danger, and the ghostlike image of an impossible love story. It was in so many ways a tragedy. But in the main, it was a ballet of hope, of wonderful promise.

And it was real. For keeps. Baryshnikov could never go home again.

In ballet, a *jeté* is a leap in which the dancer pushes off the floor with one leg, makes an arc in the air, and lands on the other leg.

Theme and Variations **was performed by Baryshnikov in 1974. The intricate Balanchine ballet was "the most difficult" he had performed since his great leap West.**

In a *grand jeté,* the dancer leaps to the highest possible elevation. His leading foot is thrust up and out, and the leg with which he pushed off the floor reaches back and up to a high extension. A near-split is sometimes achieved in a *grand jeté.*

In Baryshnikov's *grand jeté* to the West, a complete split was achieved.

The Soviet ballet star had been a guest artist with a touring troupe of Moscow's Bolshoi Ballet. On the night of his defection, he and the other members of the Bolshoi had performed in Toronto and afterward had attended a reception in their honor.

The reception lasted until the wee hours of the morning, late for dancers, who must take good care of their bodies. Ballerinas and their male partners silently and wearily made their way toward the chartered bus that would return them to their hotel.

Suddenly, Baryshnikov turned away from the others and dashed toward a darkened car waiting two blocks away. In his anxiety to reach it he was nearly run over, but the powerful legs that had carried him to such great heights on stage served him well as he fled to freedom.

Baryshnikov had abandoned the Bolshoi tour. Henceforth, his career would go forward in the West.

Witnesses to his flight say that he was pursued by members of the KGB, the Soviet secret police. If so, they never caught him. Baryshnikov leaped into the getaway car and sped away into the dark Canadian night.

Eight days later, Baryshnikov issued a statement for the benefit of the press. "When I was in Toronto," he said from a secret refuge in Mississauga, just west of Toronto, "I finally decided that if I let the opportunity of expanding my art in the West slip by, it would haunt me always."

With him in his hideout was Christina Berlin. Christina is the pretty, young daughter of Richard Berlin, who for thirty-two years was president and chief executive of the giant Hearst publishing empire.

Christina's mother called the relationship between her daughter and the Russian dancer one of friendship. "They are very good, old friends."

Mrs. Berlin had met Baryshnikov in London and dined with him and Christina. She liked and admired him.

Baryshnikov confirmed Mrs. Berlin's evaluation of his and Christina's relationship. Christina was a good, close friend, someone he could call upon to help him out in a tight spot. When things got difficult for him, he asked Christina to stand by him.

Christina was in London when Baryshnikov telephoned his appeal for help. She responded immediately. In fact, so great was her rush that she arrived at London's Heathrow Airport without cash or credit cards and had to plead with strangers to cash her personal check so she could fly to Toronto.

Relaxed after dancing in a rehearsal with Canada's National Ballet shortly after his defection, the Soviet star signed to do two guest performances with the Toronto company.

UPI Photo

Romantic ties between Christina Berlin, the American girl who comforted him after he sought asylum, and the Soviet dancer were hotly denied by Baryshnikov. They were just "good friends."

Somehow she made it.

And they were together.

But not as a romantic team.

Baryshnikov was sincere in his praise of Christina. Few people have such friends in the world. But he was equally earnest when he begged reporters not to turn the friendship into a "bedroom drama."

Nevertheless, rumors and speculations about the pair abounded. Everyone, especially the press, loves a love story.

And so, from his first steps into the West, the specter of public curiosity has dogged Baryshnikov's heels and has invaded his private life. But he is a star. In the twentieth century, stars are not allowed to have private lives.

Christina was the first in what was to be a long list of sparkling women with whom he was romantically linked.

For her part, Christina followed the party line. She adamantly denied any love affair with Baryshnikov and implored people to be concerned with his talent, not his love life.

Still, most people wanted to know more about them as a couple. They had met four years before Baryshnikov's defection when they were introduced by ballet superstar Margot Fonteyn in London during a 1970 Russian ballet tour. They hit it off right away.

Some of the people who knew them felt that the two were more than just close friends — at least as far as Christina was concerned. One of her chums described Christina as "mad about him."

Why not? Baryshnikov is a small blond Russian with soulful eyes, incredible talent, and a magnificent body.

In 1971 Christina visited him in Leningrad where he was dancing with the Kirov Ballet. But he could not leave the city and she was convinced she would never see him again. After her departure, she wrote letters to him, but they were returned, unopened.

Despairing of ever persuading Baryshnikov to leave Russia, Christina returned to New York, giving up her job as Dame Margot Fonteyn's personal assistant.

She continued to follow the movements of the Russian ballet, and pictures of the Soviet ballet star adorned the walls of her Manhattan apartment. Shunning the social set to which she belonged, Christina dated a Russian correspondent and learned to speak some Russian.

A graduate of Manhattan's exclusive Chapin School, where aspiring stars learn to perform in the dramatic arts, Christina was also an occasional student at the Actor's Studio, the famed New York acting school that nurtured the talents of such stars as Marlon Brando and Shelley Winters.

Although dedicated to learning her craft, Christina was shy and quiet, avoiding her classmates. She was also a "Russian literature freak."

In 1972 Christina returned to London. She landed a job on the London edition of *Cosmopolitan* magazine. She stayed in close touch with the ballet world through her friends and connections in the Royal Ballet.

It was not unusual for her to do so, for she had always loved the ballet. And when Baryshnikov's call for help came, Christina was ready to answer it.

Christina was not involved in the actual escape plans. Baryshnikov asked her only to be with him during a difficult time. Perhaps he needed someone familiar to talk to in a new and unfamiliar world. He needed someone to be with him during the times when his exaltation turned to sorrow. He would leap about the room, excited to be free. Then, suddenly and unexpectedly, he would burst into tears.

It was difficult not to be at home. But he realized he had to make a choice between his art and his personal happiness.

The spells of weeping continued for a time after his defection. Friends say he was also uneasy in crowds. He feared being plucked away by the Soviet secret police.

Christina was a friend, a close friend, but the closeness between the American girl who loved the ballet and the Russian boy who was to become so famous in American ballet did not blossom into a romance. Over and over again, Baryshnikov repeated for the benefit of a doubting press that Christina was a friend, only a friend.

"There is absolutely no romance."

Despite this, stories persisted about a Baryshnikov-Berlin romance until, eventually, Christina faded out of the picture. Columnists commenting on the New York social scene now wrote that the Russian dancer was escorting one dazzling girl after another. By all accounts, he had adapted to a modern American life style.

Was he happy?

Yes, most times. But the life of a defector is not always the most pleasant situation.

He had to spend too much time defending himself, his motives, and his friends from rumors and speculations. Was Natalia Makarova involved in his escape? Did she not aid in the plans for his defection? No, she was not involved.

No, it was not political.

Not political?

No!

Baryshnikov stressed that his defection was not a political act. He was not a political person, and did not wish to become one.

Was it, then, for love?

Yes.

But not for the kind of love from which young girl's dreams are made, nor the kind on which romantic ballets are constructed, all gauze and illusion. It was for a more solid and lasting kind of love, more passionate, more consuming, more demanding. It was for the love of dance.

Baryshnikov had turned to a new world, had left Russia, for his artistic growth. As an artist, it was the only decision he could make.

He explained how, in Russia, a dancer's growth is stunted. New roles are rare. Everything happens slowly in Russia and, although some artists wait, others feel they cannot wait.

At first he hoped to be able to make guest appearances, perhaps to dance in ballets by Balanchine, Tudor, Robbins, and MacMillan. Had that been allowed, he would never have left Russia.

Russian dance tradition cuts two ways. Although classical ballet is preserved best in the Soviet Union, they stick closely to the rules. They observe them rigidly.

Several conditions in the world of Soviet dance in the early 1970s contributed to Baryshnikov's leap for "artistic freedom." Among them was a "ballerina crisis" in Leningrad; this occasioned a shortage of suitable partners at the Kirov for Baryshnikov. Choreographers of first-class talent also were in short supply, and the Soviet government refused to invite Western choreographers on the grounds that it was unpatriotic.

Nor did a dancer have the freedom to choose his own repertory. And little opportunity arose for him to dance in new ballets, especially ballets created for him.

Eager and exceptionally talented, the young artist Baryshnikov yearned to work with some of the West's choreographers.

He would have stayed in Russia if that possibility had existed — had he been able to go abroad and then return to dance with the Kirov. . . . If that situation had existed, he feels that no artist would have defected from Russia.

His strong yearning to try new ballets and new choreographers, to break free of the rigid classical mold, pushed him relentlessly toward the Western door. Finally, he went through.

Defection brings "a tremendous upheaval," in the words of Remi Saunder, an interpreter who befriended Baryshnikov and became a good friend. Remi likened Baryshnikov's Russian life to that of a bird in a cage. Open the cage, and the bird will fly out. No matter how poorly it is able to fly. Remi felt that Baryshnikov had no "survival muscles." Like a bird that has lived in a cage, he had to develop them or perish.

The West welcomed Baryshnikov with open arms. He was an instant celebrity. The idea that he would be denied asylum was not even considered. What was once the Star of the East became the Star of the West. Ballet heaven was rearranged.

On July 3, 1974, the newly defected Baryshnikov received permission to remain in Canada for at least six months on a special permit. The permit, good for a year, could be renewed after the first six-month period.

He would not need the extension. Before the end of July, Baryshnikov entered the United States under an "H-1" visa. This covers nonresidents of distinguished ability.

Baryshnikov lamented the bitter price he had to pay for his change of address. In Russia he was considered a criminal. Yet he realized that not to develop his great talent would have been an even greater crime.

Before Baryshnikov left Canada, the Canadian Department of External Affairs contacted him. The Soviet Embassy in Ottawa had requested their assistance in arranging a meeting between the twenty-six-year-old artist and a Soviet representative.

A few months later, an interesting rumor was confirmed. It dealt with the unique status of the defector.

To Mother Russia, Baryshnikov was not a criminal, not a defector. He could come home. All would be forgiven, all privileges would be restored. Apparently, a great dancer is above the petty rules of the great powers.

Baryshnikov heartily agreed with the opinion of the Soviets when they declared him "not a defector." He was, rather a "selector." He had selected art over personal well-being.

No doubt, the Kirov Ballet in Leningrad would sorely miss him. He was the leading dancer in a very strong ballet company. And, with the Bolshoi's Vladimir Vasiliev, Baryshnikov was one of the two top male dancers in Russia.

All things considered — he was *the* top.

Because there was a major difference between the two dancers. Vasiliev, thirty-four, was sliding down from his peak of power. Baryshnikov, only twenty-six, was entering upon the best years of his career.

The life of a dancer is not a long one.

Baryshnikov was not the first Soviet dancer to defect. Nor was he the first defector from the Kirov Ballet. It had lost Rudolf Nureyev in 1961, and Natalia Makarova in 1970. And Valery Panov and his wife, Galina Razina, after a long, internationally publicized struggle, were allowed to emigrate to Israel just two months before Baryshnikov defected.

Despite his intention to be free of any lasting entanglements with one ballet company, Baryshnikov — through the offices of Natalia Makarova — joined the American Ballet Theatre (ABT) in New York.

Daryl Dodson, ABT's manager, proudly announced the acquisition of the Soviet dancer. He would be a guest dancer for his first season; after that, they would discuss the future.

Over the next four years — before his second defection, of sorts — Baryshnikov danced *almost* exclusively for the ABT. He also danced spectacularly.

The *New York Times* dance critic Clive Barnes called his dancing "perfect," noting the special attention he paid to style, while keeping his dancing totally free of mannerisms. Barnes raved about the athletic strength and prowess of Baryshnikov's dancing — his astounding leaps. He added that only other dancers might truly see how closely Baryshnikov approached the supposed impossible.

Russia's loss was America's gain, and dance critics in 1974 said the 26-year-old Baryshnikov might someday outrank the highly esteemed Rudolf Nureyev.

The American Ballet Theatre was an excellent choice for Baryshnikov to have made. It had repertory roles he already knew and was also able to offer him new roles.

He danced what he knew and learned what was new to him.

As the ABT began the celebration of their thirty-fifth year, they were on top of the ballet world. They had the brilliant Baryshnikov with his unusual ability to fly through the air. And they had their own incredibly talented troupe of dancers.

They also had Gelsey Kirkland, who was a wondrous talent in her own right. Gelsey had joined the company at Baryshnikov's bidding. Talent attracts talent, and there was no doubt that he was talent.

He was flash.

He was dash.

UPI Photo

He was box-office.

Only a little over a month after his arrival, all of his performances were sold out, some even before the flyers were printed. The $15, $25, and $35 seats were gone first. Still available — for a short while — were the $50, $100, and $250 seats, the ones the general public could seldom afford.

When Baryshnikov made his first appearance in Washington, D.C., in July of 1974, he was partnered with Gelsey. Theirs was a magical partnership, one that would make them celebrated throughout the dance world.

Natalia Makarova once said that a good dance partner was one who could make her fall in love with him. She meant, of course, during the time when he was dancing with her.

Four Russian expatriates share a light moment in December 1974. Galina and Valery Panov emigrated to Israel after a two-year struggle. Nureyev and Baryshnikov sought creative freedom in the U.S.

Gelsey Kirkland joined the elite corps of Balanchine's
New York City Ballet and learned the challenging steps
of *Theme and Variations* from the master himself. Once
dancing the intricate movements of the ballet she
developed tendonitis. The intense pain caused her to
consider the impossible—giving up dancing.

Photograph © Lois Greenfield

Gelsey Kirkland joined the American Ballet Theatre at Baryshnikov's bidding. And together—on stage and off—they were magic.

Maybe Gelsey felt that way, too. But her feelings were projected beyond the footlights. Baryshnikov and Kirkland became partners in more than the dance.

Whatever their offstage relationship, on stage they were beautiful. They were — to put it blandly — tremendous.

Their Washington debut was a roaring success. Audiences shouted themselves hoarse, demanding repeated curtain calls. Bouquets of flowers littered the stage of the Kennedy Opera House as the enthusiastic ballet patrons showed their appreciation.

Kirkland was twenty-one. A former principal at the New York City Ballet, the bailiwick of Balanchine, she left City Ballet to dance with the ex-Kirov star because he asked her to.

It was a decision she might later have reason to regret.

Considered America's all-around best dance company, the ABT absorbed the spectacular talents of Baryshnikov without losing its balance — a good indication of its strength.

All was not smooth sailing, however. The artist from the USSR who dived into the receptive waters of the ABT caused a few ripples in the lake of ballet harmony. Some American dancers resented the little Russian for grabbing the spotlight so completely.

Dancer Ted Kivitt said candidly that Baryshnikov's timing hurt him. At thirty-two, Kivitt looked forward to the recognition for which he had worked hard. Instead, he saw his career taking giant steps backward. No longer would he be the star.

ABT ballerina Cynthia Gregory concurred. She felt that, as an American, she could offer nothing but her dancing. Yet, no matter how well she danced, she would not be awarded the recognition given to the Russian stars.

It is doubtful that anyone at the ABT resented the talent that Baryshnikov brought with him, however. Besides, he brought with him his Kirov schooling, classical perfection, and a stunning display of technical virtuosity. All of which he was willing to share.

Baryshnikov was open. Open to new ideas, new friendships. He wasn't afraid of taking risks or failing in new roles. And he took special pains to be just another member of the gang.

He was energy.

He was art.

But he was nevertheless resented.

No matter that it wasn't his fault if fame followed him around like his pet poodle. He didn't encourage that sort of attention (except from his dog). But it is hard to say that fame is wrong.

Talent should be recognized. How much better off would many of the world's now-famous artists have been if fame had accompanied their respective talents?

Consider everyone's favorite example, the artist Van Gogh.

In any case, press attention is not easily discouraged once it has spotted a personality worthy of the fuss. This is especially true in the center of the media, New York City. In the dance capital of the world, the media would pursue Baryshnikov.

But on the plus side for the ballet star, the media were also available to him, for his enjoyment and education. He eagerly investigated American plays, operas, and films. He especially appreciated television, watching all the old movies. He became a student of TV.

The pressure of life in New York bothered Baryshnikov, the furious speed with which New Yorkers burn up their time. He described the tempo in the Big Apple as ten times faster than it had been in Leningrad. He once commented that he liked Paris because "people have more time there than in New York."

Then, too, there was the language barrier. Although he spoke other languages besides Russian, in English Baryshnikov was not fluent.

Even so, it was "love at first sight." And in New York, coping with his new life and the pangs of separation from his home, Baryshnikov "became a man."

Surrogate parents helped him over the first hurdles: Remi Saunder and Howard Gilman, board chairman of the Gilman Paper Company.

Gilman, a patron of music and dance, lent Baryshnikov a Manhattan penthouse apartment rent-free. He and Remi Saunder introduced Baryshnikov to such artists as Mstislav Rostropovich and conductor Leonard Bernstein.

Rostropovich, also Russian, acclaimed as the greatest cellist in the world, was living in temporary exile. Baryshnikov and he had a common ground on which to meet and talk. They could discuss their homeland, which Baryshnikov sorely missed.

He would emphasize that he liked New York. Yet he could not call it home. To him, Leningrad always would be home.

It was hard — most painful — for Baryshnikov not to be able to return to Russia. Especially in the last few years at the Kirov, the management had been very good to him.

He had loved the Kirov and it had given him much. At times he wondered if he had made a mistake. Then he would see that he must take advantage of his opportunity in America.

"Anyway, what's done is done. There is no going back."

Photograph © Lois Greenfield

Prima ballerina Natalia Makarova, a defector in 1970, helped young Mikhail adjust to the American ballet world.

Entrée
Russian Roots

The *entrée,* or opening passages, in the life of the future ballet idol Mikhail Baryshnikov, began quietly in Riga, Latvia, on January 27, 1948. Like Balanchine's ballet *Theme and Variations,* his life had an understated beginning, full of serenity and peaceful grandeur. It also had moments of latent tension and restless energy — building up and up and up toward the inevitable climax.

Mikhail's parents were Russian. His father was an engineer, his mother a dressmaker. Tow-headed Mikhail's first childhood memory is of a sunny day in Riga.

He and his mother were outside. Unable to walk well as yet, he held on to her skirt for support. He remembers the dress she was wearing — a chiffon dress with yellow and purple flowers. To the young Mikhail, his mother, an ash-blond with bright blue eyes, was incredibly beautiful in the sunlight.

Baryshnikov's homeland is noted less for sunlight than for snow and vodka. But it is sunlight he remembers.

In 1969—five years before his defection—the Soviet star acknowledged the applause at the First International Competition for ballet dancers in Moscow.

Located in northern Eurasia and stretching from the Baltic to the Pacific, Russia lies three-fourths in Asia, the remainder in Europe.

To the west are Romania, Hungary, Czechoslovakia, Poland, Finland, and Norway. To the north is the Arctic Ocean. To the east is the great Pacific. To the south lie Korea, China, Mongolia, Afghanistan, Iran, and Turkey.

In area, Russia is the world's largest country, covering one-sixth of all land surface.

Latvia, where Baryshnikov was born, is one of the group of socialist republics within the Soviet Union. Technically the inhabitants of Latvia are Latvians, not Russians; but Baryshnikov's parents were Russian citizens, so Mikhail was Russian.

Latvia, with a population of approximately two and one-half million, is about the size of West Virginia, and has about the same population. Latvia was handed over to Stalin by Hitler as part of the German-Soviet Nonaggression pact that preceded World War II. The country was again taken over by Germany in 1941 and retaken by Russia in 1945. The Soviets retained Latvia after the war.

Despite all claims to the contrary, there is a class system in Russia. An upper class, a middle class, a lower blue-collar class, and a farming class are ascertainable. Although the Soviet class system is not based on inherited wealth or the private ownership of property, as is true in the United States, the Soviet classes are based on essentially the same things as those in America — status and power.

The upper class is composed of government bureaucrats (about six hundred thousand of them) who run the government and society. In the middle class are the specialists and professionals including writers, artists, high-level university professors, and scientists. The lower classes — as is often the case — are made up of farmers and manual laborers.

Baryshnikov was firmly in the middle class.

Both powerful nations, Russia and the United States share certain qualities. Courage, energy, and humor can be found in the citizens of both countries. But the countries are different. Russians and Americans have different mentalities and take different psychological approaches to life and living.

Decisions are reached differently, too. And, of course, the politics of the two countries are definitely in opposition. Thus Americans and Russians often find it hard to understand each other.

Yet, when he was growing up, Mikhail thought little of all that. He skipped along the shores of the ancient Baltic Sea and had a very happy childhood. He ran, leaped, swam, and kicked a football. He was an active child. He hated to sit still.

Besides football, he tried fencing and gymnastics. He even sang in the children's choir.

He tried piano lessons, too. He modestly says he was "very bad."

Bad or not, his childhood dream was to be a concert pianist and play with a large orchestra. His mother changed that dream — and ballet history — when she took her energetic young son to the Latvian Opera School to take the entrance exam.

Baryshnikov recalls that he liked it right away. Theater interested him from the start.

Mikhail was twelve at the time, a relatively late age for a dancer to begin his study. Most serious students start at age seven or eight.

He admits he did not take dancing seriously at first. His was more the interest of a dilettante. Soon, however, he began to glimpse the challenge dancing held for him.

He had tried many sports and at one time wanted to be a gymnast. But he hated discipline. And although good at school academically, he found it hard to sit still in school.

With this temperament, dancing was difficult for him to study seriously. But he liked the challenge.

The ballet was not particularly understandable for the twelve-year-old Mikhail, but the mystery dared him. Dared him to understand with both his mind and his body.

By the end of his first year of training, all his other activities became secondary. They would soon disappear altogether. Dancing would replace all else. After his first performance, he couldn't tear himself away from the ballet.

Most exciting was the reaction of the audience.

Gradually, the difficulty of learning eased.

He wanted to learn and had very good teachers. He saw it as a great chance — maybe his last. Before he was fourteen, he knew what he was working for. By sixteen, dancing was a necessary part of his life.

Tragedy entered his life when he was thirteen. His mother died.

His father remarried soon after.

Perhaps this trauma in his life made him turn to the ballet as a solace for his grief. Dancing was what his mother had led him to. And it was a comfort to him.

The raw energy dance consumed could take his mind away from the emptiness in his heart. He was forced to concentrate on the physical stress he was imposing on his body.

And he danced. And he danced.

The dance, something he liked, became something he loved.

Besides dancing, he studied French and other subjects — many of

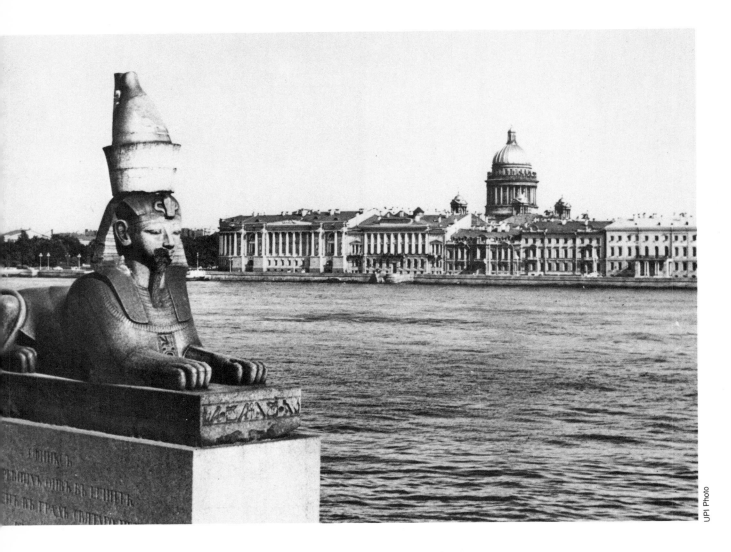

UPI Photo

Stately buildings comprising the Admiralty line the banks of the Neva River, which flows through Leningrad. Cut by numerous canals and streams, the city has more than six hundred bridges.

them relating to the ballet. The Latvian Opera School had then — and still has — high scholastic ranking.

At fifteen, Mikhail was invited to join a troupe of dancers who toured and performed for teen-agers.

A stop on the tour brought the adolescent Mikhail to the old Czarist capital of Leningrad, formerly Saint Petersburg. The classic charm of the city was like heady wine or good Russian vodka.

He wanted to stay.

He strolled down Nevsky-Prospekt, one of the most famous avenues in the world. The Hermitage was there, full of treasures. The Winter Palace. The Cathedral of Saint Isaac.

He had to stay.

Perhaps this strong desire to live in Leningrad gave the young man the courage to do what he did next.

He applied for admission to the famed Kirov School of Ballet.

The Kirov had nurtured such greats as Nijinsky, Pavlova, Karsavina,

UPI Photo

Danilova, Balanchine, and Nureyev, all of whom were giants in the history of world ballet.

Alexander Pushkin, who taught at the Kirov school, was one of the greatest of all Russian male ballet teachers. He had also been the teacher of Nureyev, who had defected three years before Mikhail applied to study at the Kirov. The two great dancers were not to meet until they were introduced in New York in 1974.

When he attended a dance class at the Kirov school, young Mikhail was overwhelmed by the desire to be a Kirov student. He approached Pushkin and said simply, "I would very much like to be your pupil."

The great Pushkin allowed the boy to dance for him.

"I was like a young goat knocking over tables and chairs," Baryshnikov recalls.

But Pushkin studied the boy carefully, then took him downstairs to the school's doctors. They checked him over thoroughly, the way they would a race horse. They probed and poked.

Pedestrian and auto traffic are heavy along famed Nevsky-Prospekt, a main shopping area in Russia's second largest city, the beloved home of Mikhail Baryshnikov.

Apparently they liked what they found, for Baryshnikov was admitted to the Kirov School of Ballet. Personable, full of good humor, and bursting with talent, the young man's potential was obvious.

Admittance was not to be immediate, however. He had to spend the summer in Riga awaiting final approval.

Baryshnikov says that it would have been "shattering" if he had not been accepted. He spent the summer mentally living the life of the Kirov. Leningrad and the school alike were electrifying for him. He could not imagine living apart from them.

He tried to relax by fishing — a sport he still enjoys — but it is doubtful that his heart was totally running with the fish that anxious summer.

He waited.

Then came word to gladden his soul. He was accepted.

Pushkin taught only a few boys at a time, and young Baryshnikov was to be one of them. He had been accepted into the Kirov school, into Pushkin's "class of perfection."

It was wonderful for Baryshnikov. He acquired an excellent start toward the mastery of classical dance, ballet history, acting, mime, and fencing in the three years he boarded at the Kirov.

He also acquired a nickname — Misha. The name was given to him by Pushkin, and today Baryshnikov is generally and affectionately known as Misha to his friends and fans.

Misha sometimes lived with Pushkin and his wife. He became almost a son to the teacher; in turn, Misha looked upon the Pushkins as his family, for his own mother was dead, and his father lived far away in Riga.

But, above all, Misha was a student, a student of the legendary Pushkin.

It was a great responsibility even to be Pushkin's student, for Pushkin was acknowledged as a great teacher. A Pushkin student who could not do a step had no one but himself to blame.

Misha, and the other students, worked from nine in the morning until ten at night. Sweating, straining, and stretching tight muscles. Misha continued his studies in French and to them added makeup, and Russian and Western literature.

The Kirov school is famous for its instruction in acting although, by Western standards, the acting is highly stylized. The Kirov instructors are especially noted for their skill in teaching mime.

At the age of eighteen, Baryshnikov was admitted to the full Kirov regimen. By that time he had spent three years in Pushkin's "class of perfection."

Misha was assigned to solo roles without having to fight his way up through the ranks of apprentices who serve in the corps de ballet, which

The good-humored, immensely likable ballet idol acquired the nickname Misha from his great teacher Pushkin at the Kirov Ballet school.

is the chorus of a ballet company.

This was a highly unusual move — one reserved only for the best. Nijinsky (considered one of the finest male dancers who ever lived), Pavlova, and Nureyev were predecessors of Baryshnikov who shared this high esteem.

A state-supported organization with a company of more than two hundred dancers, the Kirov had a repertory at the time of Baryshnikov's leaving of only twenty-six ballets — small by Western standards.

Because they had so few ballets and so many dancers, and because in Russia the theater must share space with the opera, Baryshnikov danced only three or four times a month.

Nevertheless, in 1967, when he was only nineteen, tales of the Russian whirlwind who commanded the stage and leaped to incredible heights began to be told in the West. On a trip to the Soviet Union that year, the dance critic Clive Barnes described the talented Misha as an *almost* flawless dancer.

Barnes felt the young dancer lacked the strength that would come with age. He also found Baryshnikov's dancing less exciting than some. But he recognized in Misha "a dancer of whom the world will hear more."

The five-foot, seven-inch boy wonder performed hypnotically. Barnes noted that more "attention was drawn to the strange, serious-looking boy than I had ever seen before." The fair hair, the frown of intense concentration, the "unaffected perfection" were all recorded.

In 1970 Baryshnikov danced for Western audiences for the first time — in London and again in the Netherlands. He was enthusiastically acclaimed. His performances away from home were a triumph.

But not completely.

His tastes, it was noted, ran to Western clothing and Western women. This was not something to be applauded by the political leadership in the USSR. It was something with which to be concerned.

Baryshnikov felt the baleful stare of disapproving Soviet eyes.

He was watched.

In 1970 there was also tragedy in store for him.

His teacher, Pushkin, died.

Baryshnikov was to be his last great pupil. And the young artist was to miss Pushkin sorely. Of his teacher he said he was "a pure and simple character."

Baryshnikov respected Pushkin immensely, comparing him to "somebody who stepped out of an icon." He indicated that it was Pushkin who turned his love of dance into a passion.

Describing Pushkin as "a father to me," Baryshnikov recalled his teacher as a man with "amazing gentleness and sensitivity, a desire to help his students." Above all, said Baryshnikov, "he was a person."

The classes that Pushkin taught had not been noticeably different from others' classes. But the great teacher had — through inherent ability and sheer work experience — become so steeped in his profession that he wore it like a second skin.

He steered rather than pushed his students, and he never forced a dancer to do what he didn't want to do. He brought out the best in each dancer, but he took no credit for it. His students' successes belonged to them, not to Pushkin.

Pushkin died in the streets of Leningrad in 1970. Saddened by the loss of his friend and teacher — his "almost father" — Baryshnikov transformed his sorrow into positive action. He offered to take over Pushkin's class.

He was permitted to do so.

Misha tried to pass on what he had been taught, "the most logical series of steps and movements" he had ever seen.

Would Baryshnikov have left Russia if Pushkin had not died?

Who knows? Only Baryshnikov. And he has not supplied the answer.

But it seems logical to assume that Pushkin's death made it easier for Misha to leave. There was no longer anything to hold him back. His mother was dead; he was not close to his father (geographically, at any rate); now, Pushkin was gone.

For seven years before his defection, Baryshnikov was the ballet idol of the Soviet Union. He was the youngest performer ever to receive the State Award of Merit. In 1966, when he was eighteen, he won the gold medal at the Varna international competition in Bulgaria. He repeated his triumph in 1969 in Moscow.

In 1969 a ballet solo was created for him. Choreographer Leonid Jacobson composed *Vestris*. In the solo, Baryshnikov portrayed the great eighteenth-century French dancer Auguste Vestris, who has been called the God of Dance.

A fitting role for Misha.

In his daily life Baryshnikov did not act the part of rebel. He made no trouble. He had little reason to do so, actually. He made a good salary and had a fine apartment, a maid, and other fringe benefits, including a car. He lived well.

Still, it wasn't enough.

Although he had everything the system could offer him, it wasn't easy for him.

Dances he wished to dance, music he wanted to set to choreography, did not conform to the official taste of the ideology committee. They were "not suitable for the ballet."

Photograph © Lois Greenfield

Photograph © Lois Greenfield

Theme and Variations, in Balanchine's
neo-classical style, demands strict
control and enormous power from the
dancers. Baryshnikov found the strain on
his legs "incredible."

There was also a certain lack of spice in his life. As Remi Saunder put it, "There you are given food, but not a choice of food."

Russian artists are treated very well materially, but they have little chance to experience the natural highs and lows that come with the use of one's own initiative.

Still, it must have come as a shock to the KGB when the ballet idol "who had everything" decided to scratch the itch in his feet and wander off to foreign lands, to see what lay far beyond the Urals.

He had everything. They must have asked themselves: what more could he want?

Not fame, certainly. He had that.

Not adoration, either. He had that, too. In Leningrad he was besieged by women who worshiped him.

And it wasn't for great honor. Weeks before he defected, a gala was held at the Kirov, and a whole evening of dance was dedicated to him.

He danced three new ballets.

But other things were not so nice. One of his favorite roles was *The Creation of the World,* which was based on drawings by Jean Effel. In it, Baryshnikov danced seminude.

"*Nyet!*" cried the cultural minister. "Is too sexy. Is too trivial."

It was back to the drawing board for *The Creation of the World.* The ballet must adhere to official taste. And the spectrum of artistic approval was extremely narrow.

The artist within Baryshnikov burned.

He had suffered silently and stoically over minor irritations. But to be censored artistically was a *divertissement.* A dance without plot. Without message. A dance of form only.

In vain he tried to say that ballet changes constantly, that generations change. Limitations, too, should change.

Art, Baryshnikov believes, should be above politics. The language of art is a common language. Audiences are the same everywhere in the world. When the dancing is good, audiences are enthusiastic, no matter what country you are in.

So Mikhail Baryshnikov, dancer *extraordinaire,* left his homeland, for art's sake, and proceeded to conquer the Western dance world.

He could see how Natalia Makarova and Rudolf Nureyev had grown as artists after they left Russia. He, too, wished to grow.

The finely honed precision of his classical Russian training is beautifully apparent in this shot of Misha performing in *Theme and Variations*.

The Reluctant Celebrity
Pas d'action

It is probably unfair, and certainly downright frivolous, but Mikhail "Misha" Baryshnikov is better known to the American public for his natural, unaffected predilection for beautiful women than for his fantastic technical skill in the performance of ballet.

Well, that's not exactly true.

Not any longer.

Now he is best known for his role of Yuri in *The Turning Point,* a role for which he won an Oscar nomination.

He was amazed. For acting?

Is joke, no?

If they had given him the nomination for dancing, well, that would be a different story. But for acting?

He thought of the role as good experience. But he is not a professional actor. He compared his being picked for the part with the old story of the director who makes a star out of someone with a photogenic face and a stronger-than-usual personality.

Judith Jamison of Alvin Ailey's City Center Dance Theater does the "Hustle" with Misha on a Manhattan penthouse terrace. They were announcing their upcoming dance alliance to photographers and reporters.

He was shocked when he saw his first rushes.

He felt he was terrible. But Herb Ross, the film's director, reassured him when he said all actors who look at rushes for the first time are horrified.

The film, of course, added greatly to Misha's celebrity status outside the close-knit world of ballet. Baryshnikov found himself a superstar.

Nora Kaye, the former ballerina who is married to Herb Ross, predicted that Baryshnikov would get other offers to act.

"I wonder if he will take them," she mused.

Yes, he is definitely a superstar. But does he like it?

He is living, he says, his own life. If people stop him on the streets or send him letters, what can he do?

Nevertheless, he confesses that at times it bothers him very much.

Which is probably an understatement.

Baryshnikov is a serious man — albeit the seriousness is laced with a strong shot of humor — and if he could have his way, he probably would prefer being left alone.

For sure, he had said often enough that he would not mind it one bit if the press let him be. If the hullabaloo were not so noisy or so undignified.

Robert Redford once courageously informed a roomful of reporters that he was not a public person. He felt that the fact that he was an actor did not mean that he must automatically share his private life with the public.

"I owe the public a performance," he said, and added that it's up to them to decide whether they like it or not. His private life he considered his own.

Well, perhaps.

Perhaps not.

Can you separate the artist from his art? The dancer from the dance?

In any case, Baryshnikov's activities, and speculations about his activities, appeared regularly in the press. Not only in gossip columns and scandal sheets, either. In the "respectable" press.

He is the "Travolta of High Culture," bannered *People* magazine.

His "blue-gray eyes have 'an over-ripe' look and hint at unreported night-time activity," said *New York* magazine.

A writer for the *New York Times* claimed Baryshnikov's eyes gave "mute testimony to too much work or unknown night-time pleasures."

He likes to play, reported *Time* magazine in its 1975 cover story. *Time* noted that, despite Baryshnikov's revelation that he is drawn to "sad ballets, sad feelings," he can be the life of a party.

Well, he plays the piano and is an excellent mimic. And once, at a party for the ABT in Texas, he and several other male dancers skinny-dipped in the pool. When a young woman dancer entered the pool, he led the group that helped her take off her bathing suit.

He is basically one of the guys. He will wait his turn for a shower, buy champagne for a special occasion, and join in any celebration. He eases tension by humorous diversions, such as belting out a rousing rendition of show tunes, or just playing the fool. He uses his excellent ability as a mimic to make people laugh. He loves harmless practical jokes like blackening his teeth, as he did as Yuri in *The Turning Point.*

But, despite this openness, this desire to see people happy and relaxed, he is alone much of the time. He compares himself to a "wolf lost from the pack."

He is so busy that he has made very few good friends. He feels that it takes years to develop deep friendships.

He is no longer afraid that if he answers a knock at his door late at night, he will be whisked away by the secret police. He is no longer afraid in crowds. Still, he is most comfortable in the company of other Russian émigrés, in the intimate setting of small dinner parties.

Baryshnikov, the movie star, jokes with co-star Leslie Browne in a scene from *The Turning Point.* Both were nominated for Oscars for their debut performances.

At home he plays the stereo, recites Russian poetry — Pasternak, Mandelstam, Pushkin (no relation to his teacher) — and laughs at Florence Foster Jenkins's eccentric operatic high-jinks.

He does not cook. He claims that standing at a stove would be "terrible" for his legs.

He drinks vodka, Scotch and soda, or Heineken beer.

He is an occasional smoker, but he is trying to cut down.

Partial to French, Russian, and hot Chinese Szechwan dishes, he also likes American steak and salad.

Sweets are not for him.

Offstage he is sometimes moody. Brooding. His personality has been known to change abruptly. His sunny disposition is suddenly obscured by dark gray clouds of gloom. He becomes quiet, withdrawn.

He loves dogs. He was heartbroken when he had to leave his dog behind in the Soviet Union. He now has a large black poodle, which he calls La Goulue, after the notorious dancer who was one of Toulouse-Lautrec's favorite subjects.

Louise Weber was the real name of the blonde Alsatian laundress who reached fame and notoriety at the Moulin Rouge. One of Lautrec's most famous posters, that of the strawberry blonde in the brown and white polka-dotted blouse, kicking up her heels, is of La Goulue.

Baryshnikov has been overheard referring playfully to his poodle as a "dirty garbage rat" as he tickles her ears.

Misha is adorable, talented, and also one of the most highly paid dancers in the world. It's little wonder that many women desire him. He radiates sexiness, onstage and off.

Is that a nice feeling?

He admits that, for him, it is "important."

Perhaps it is at that.

But he does not care to be asked about how it feels to be a sex symbol. Questions dealing with that taboo subject go unanswered — usually. And a storm brews behind the cool blue eyes.

He makes no secret of the fact that he "adores women." When asked his opinion of American women, he describes them as "much tougher than usual."

And then he qualifies that statement. "Tougher" is the wrong word. He means "much stronger mentally."

Does he, then, like stronger women — mentally?

Ummmm.

He admits he likes the "image of energy" stamped on American women. That is, he likes it up to a "normal" level. He does not mean women in "leather jackets."

There are gaggles of women who don't wear leather jackets, and Baryshnikov's name is kept alive in the gossip columns by their attention to him. Or vice versa.

One pundit, terming Baryshnikov the year's hot young superstar, added that "he always gets the girl."

Baryshnikov complains that his private life has become some sort of symbol. "I'm not the first straight dancer, nor the last," he protests.

He certainly is not.

But he is the most vivid, the best known. He is — to most — the epitome of the masculine ballet dancer.

Edward Villella, a principal at the New York City Ballet, did a great deal toward breaking the stereotyped image of the effeminate male ballet dancer. And this was long before Baryshnikov entered the scene.

Villella came to the dance indirectly. His first love was sports. He was injured while playing in a sandlot baseball game. His sister's ballet classes would offer more supervision, his mother felt.

He studied until he was fifteen. Then he went to the New York State Maritime College, earning a Bachelor of Science degree in marine transportation, playing baseball, and becoming the campus welterweight boxing champion.

He returned to dancing as therapy after a barroom injury.

This time, he was serious about his dancing. He joined the City Ballet in 1957, when he was twenty, and became a principal.

And he proceeded through a great ballet career.

Villella at one time was a part owner of the discothèque Arthur, and he heartily enjoyed his bachelorhood after his seven-year marriage to Janet Greschler broke up. His ex-wife — who is also an ex-dancer — and he have one child, Roddy, age nine.

But it was Baryshnikov, not Villella, who reached far into the hinterlands of America and changed the ballet dancer's image for all time.

"You know what this fantastic little Russian is going to do? He's going to make it respectable for American boys to be dancers." So says a character in *The Turning Point*.

If that line was not written about Baryshnikov, it could have been.

When you ask him about the image assigned to him by the public, he indicates that the role does not please him.

It is a terrible cliché, he claims, that ballet dancers are thought of as being homosexual. It has no relevance, anyway.

Who cares? is the viewpoint of Baryshnikov. To him, dancers, like anyone else, should live their lives in the way they want. And be happy. That's it.

He states firmly that he is responsible only for himself.

He does not want to discuss "right" and "wrong." He is not a lawyer or clergyman.

But he certainly doesn't hide the fact that he likes women.

"This is not worst reputation," he adds.

No. But, for a ballet dancer, it is unusual.

Dancer Ted Kivitt agrees that it *shouldn't* matter what the sexual preference of a dancer is, but he knows that the stigma still exists.

Kivitt thinks things have changed somewhat, but a male in the ballet is still stigmatized. He recalls that when he asked his girl to marry him, her brother flew up from Texas to meet him. Says Kivitt, "He had his doubts."

After brother and brother-in-law-to-be met, the union between Ted Kivitt and Karena Brock, both principals at the ABT, was fully approved.

Obviously, and as is true for the rest of the population, there are different life styles for different dancers.

Baryshnikov's life style, for instance, is unrestricted by matrimonial ties.

He has conducted affairs with many women, often with dancers he has worked with. And some of these friendships have ended with chilly abruptness.

Misha, it has been said, rapidly worked his way through the corps de ballet at the American Ballet Theatre. Left strewn in his wake were brokenhearted would-be Giselles. Lately, Hollywood stars are said to be succumbing to his abundant charm.

Has the young Romeo from Riga really left a trail of broken hearts as he worked his way through the ranks?

A former ballerina girl friend of Misha's admitted that she, like others before her, knew the relationship wouldn't last, but added pensively, "Who could resist?"

Gelsey Kirkland apparently was one who couldn't.

The ballerina Misha once compared to a finely cut polished diamond — one of the most exciting ballerinas dancing today — joined him as his partner at the ABT.

Gelsey had met Misha in 1972 when she was touring with a City Ballet company through Russia. She saw him perform there. In the summer of 1974 she journeyed to Toronto to watch the Bolshoi, with which Misha was performing. At supper afterward, they renewed their brief acquaintance and grew to like each other.

Gelsey was an ideal size to be partnered with Baryshnikov. Her "almost five-foot-four" is a neat match for his "almost five-foot-seven."

And she was definitely talented enough to be his partner.

Perhaps the thought of a possible partnership entered Baryshnikov's mind at that time.

Gelsey and Mikhail dance the *pas de deux* (a dance for two) from *Don Quixote* with the Pennsylvania Ballet Company at the Brooklyn Academy of Music. Mikhail loves this "crazy Russian salad of a ballet."

UPI Photo

Above & right: As the lusty, high-spirited barber, Basil, Baryshnikov woos the innkeeper's daughter, Kitri. The romance between Kirkland and Baryshnikov sparkled on stage and off.

Perhaps it entered her mind also.

When Gelsey received a call from one of Baryshnikov's associates asking her to dance with him, now that he had elected not to return to the Soviet Union, she was instantly receptive.

Would she dance with him?

"Of course I will!"

And she did.

Onstage — together — they dazzled. Offstage — together — they were electric. The togetherness turned into a love affair.

Gelsey, perhaps as dedicated in the pursuit of perfection in their common art as Baryshnikov, held her own opinions about professionalism in dance. Some of her views differed from Baryshnikov's. High-voltage discussions ensued about individual approaches to technique and style.

Perhaps this professional tension contributed to the eventual breakup. In any case, Misha — like the character Yuri in *The Turning Point* — moved on to others.

The parting hurt her.

But Gelsey recovered.

She recovered not only from the break with Baryshnikov, but from other problems as well. She suffered through a weight problem (at one time she weighed less than 90 pounds), which caused her to lose the ballerina role in *The Turning Point* to Leslie Browne. She also went through a frustrating psychological conflict about her feelings for the ballet. She both loved the dance and resented it. The opposing emotions were pulling her apart. But rewarding sessions with physical therapists, physicians, and dance teachers helped her to pull her act together. Today Gelsey is better adjusted and more respected than she has ever been, winning praise from both Baryshnikov ("she advances from performance to performance") and Rudolf Nureyev ("she has that beautiful fluidity in her movements and an incredible strength for such a small girl").

She also moved on to a pleasant, comfortable relationship with tall, blond ABT soloist Richard Schafer.

There is no reason whatsoever to blame Baryshnikov for any of Gelsey's problems. Even as a little girl Gelsey was headstrong and determined to take on the world.

Her mother, joking about Gelsey's grit and drive, once said her daughter had come out of the womb marching.

Nor was Baryshnikov responsible for Gelsey's disappointment after the bright flame of their relationship flickered and went out.

He says with a sigh, "I make no promises."

Another of Baryshnikov's non-ballet occupations is reading. Aleksandr Solzhenitsyn is a writer whose books fill him with emotion — a sense of awe and *tristesse,* a sweet sadness.

And, of course, he likes Russian poetry.

Mandelstam, one of his favorite poets, wrote the following lines in his poem *Tristia:*

> I've learned the science of farewells — at night
> When those unloosened-hair laments are wept. . . .

Undoubtedly, Baryshnikov has enjoyed the sad feelings the poem evokes, and has perhaps pondered the significance of the final lines:

> We shall remember even in Lethe's cold
> That Earth cost us as much as ten heavens.

Perhaps he has also pondered and enjoyed the poem *The Key,* which was written by an anonymous Russian poet. It's a hearty Russian borscht of a poem. Full of life, but tinted with the beet-red melancholy of a heavy heart.

I was a bachelor — I lived by myself.
I had a room with a private door.
And whenever I got in a certain mood,
I invited a visitor.
My friends lived with their mothers-in-law
And with wives from the same grain . . .
Either too fat or too thin,
Monotonous and gray like rain.
And every year — having aged one year
Bearing kids of either sex,
The wives became statues in long bread lines
With nooses around their necks.
And all my friends loved their wives;
They used to ask me this:
Why don't you marry? You Playboy, You!
What do you know of married bliss?
My friends didn't like their wives;
They liked girls with soft, young hands
And with eyes into which like a stone one falls,
And falls and falls and never lands.
I was squeamish (you remember, no doubt)
I didn't ask stupid questions; I knew how to behave . . .
I simply gave them the key to my room;
That's what they asked for — and that's what I gave.

What do they see in him, this ballet Adonis? How do those ladies who adore him describe him?

"He's a dream," says one.

"He's wonderful," says another.

Yet, one's first impression can be disappointing. He seems chunky, his muscles are overdeveloped, and he has a somewhat rounded back. Nor does he have the magnetism of a Rudolf Nureyev.

He may lack the electric personality of Nureyev, but women do not seem to miss it.

"Stripped of stage make-up, he looks even younger and more vulnerable, with pale skin and those huge, dreamy eyes," cooed Joanna Ney in *Cosmopolitan.*

Women all see the same man, at least the essence of the same man. And in that essence, he is Prince Charming.

His short stature doesn't matter — not even to tall women — and certainly not to petite, lacelike ballerinas. Ballerinas such as Leslie Browne.

Leslie co-starred with Misha in *The Turning Point,* and rumors of a romance between the two flew about the movie set. Then she watched as Baryshnikov showed up with actress Jessica Lange at a party thrown to celebrate the end of filming.

Like a typical Aquarian (he was born under the sun sign Aquarius), Baryshnikov does not seem the type to settle down with one woman.

Aquarians don't take to marriage too readily, according to the astrologers. Most of them "avoid it as long as it's humanly possible," says Linda Goodman in her popular book on astrology, *Sun Signs.*

Aquarians are always seeking — one more experience, one more experiment. But they are also known to have high ideals. Perhaps this is why they desire change and are often controversial.

What does Aquarian Baryshnikov enjoy besides the ballet, poetry, and women? What would he do if he weren't a dancer? If it gets to the point where he can no longer dance?

He doesn't know. He thinks he might enjoy raising dogs. He likes fishing. He can see himself involved in the business end of ballet. . . .

At present, however, "dancing is a necessity for me."

He doesn't want to make any more movies. Not now.

An interesting director and an interesting subject might well change his mind. He cannot say he will never make another film. Who knows?

He has not, for all time, ruled out the possibility. But his enthusiasm for films is not at fever pitch.

Part of the reason for not wanting to make another movie may be his reaction to his first film. He cannot shake the feeling of strangeness he experienced.

Filming is very difficult for a dancer. There is too much waiting, too much stillness.

He found it interesting meeting professional and talented actresses such as Anne Bancroft and Shirley MacLaine. And watching them work.

But he found it difficult dancing in front of a camera.

He also found it hard to keep his dancer's body in shape. Some days the shooting went on from seven in the morning until midnight.

There was also the bureaucratic chain of command to contend with. Everything that went on in the filming involved unions, and in order to have a successful, cooperative crew, the threads between unions and producers had to be tightly interwoven. If one weak thread broke, the whole cloth unraveled.

Last, but certainly not least, there was the language problem.

Misha's mind must work with computerlike efficiency for him to speak his lines correctly, translating English to Russian to English. Unless he can grasp the point of phrases, it is just so much phonetics.

He must know the meaning! There he goes again, being a perfectionist. Deciding to do something, then doing his best.

But it all paid off, and he received high praise from director Herb Ross.

Ross thinks Baryshnikov has already made the transition from dancer to actor. He recognized how nervous the dancer was during the first read-through of the script. But Ross also saw "the intelligence and instincts of a superior artist." Baryshnikov realized that there was a huge difference between projecting a role on stage and behaving more naturally in front of a camera. He also knew how to improvise. And his ability to ad lib was a tremendous advantage.

Somehow, in spite of the many problems, the whole project blended together and the company brought forth a masterpiece, a multicolored tapestry.

Not flawless, but beautiful.

Even in the distinguished company of the cast of *The Turning Point,* the dancer who played Yuri stood out.

Herb Ross called it "wit and charm in the movie sense." This opinion was rousingly seconded by critics, audiences, and the Oscar-nominating committee.

But Baryshnikov does not care much about that praise. He cares only about his image as a dancer, and about what his friends think of him.

He knows he cannot care about the whole world.

Yet, despite the hounding of fame, all the futile attempts to open his heart for publication, he says he is happy — and lucky.

"I am the luckiest man."

Maybe he is.

The Artist
Danseur Noble

You do not observe Baryshnikov the first time you see him dance — you absorb him. He is unique. Dazzling. Unbelievable. Positively overwhelming.

He is a genius, and like all geniuses, he conjures up his magical reality from a bubbling blend of 99 percent perspiration and one percent inspiration. A potent combination.

There may be some luck involved, but hardly enough to be noticed. In the main, dancing is dedicated hard work.

Baryshnikov recognized this as a student. It was a hard job, he says. "Job" may be the wrong word for what he does, but whatever you do, says Misha, "you should do it best."

And he does it best.

The impish, pale smooth face highlighted by soft blond hair and Baltic blue eyes conceals a computer-sharp mind. For it is behind those eyes with their dark, dramatic shadows, inside his head, that the control center of the superb athlete's body lies. The sharp intelligence that is the driver sits there.

In 1976, Baryshnikov did something "really new"—Twyla Tharp's *Push Comes to Shove*. The off-balance movement of the ballet was utterly foreign to his classically trained body.

And a masterful driver it must be to control the jumps, the stops, the 180-degree turns, the *cabrioles,* and *grands ballonnés,* the *grands jetés.* The extraordinary way he seems to hover in midair.

How does he do it?

"It's normal," he says, shrugging it off, disdainful of the long preparation involved, the extreme effort needed.

To Baryshnikov, the steps are just classical steps. Although they are difficult, he treats them almost as commonplace: "You see them all the time."

The height of his jumps, how many turns he does, or how fast he can do them — that is not the point.

The *grand jeté,* in fact, is not one of his favorite steps. And he complains that the public is insatiable. They want more and more.

Does he do ten pirouettes now? Perhaps next year he will do twelve.

He is afraid the public thinks of him as a machine.

Yet no one could accuse Misha of being a machine. The life he exudes could not come from such an objective entity. But his body is a finely honed, precisely tuned instrument. In that sense, he *is* a machine, a magnificent machine.

He came to the dance physically prepared, having flirted with gymnastics, but the long, grueling hours of energy-filled time he spent in classes really shaped and strengthened his body. It gave him the physical skills he needed, the skills he now displays with such seeming ease.

He is the greatest male classical dancer of his day.

He may be the greatest dancer ever.

In execution Baryshnikov combines a rare blend of two kinds of dancers.

The first displays the nuts and bolts and underpinnings of his craft.

The second makes it all seem effortless, concealing the workings under a solid chassis of smoothly flowing lines.

Baryshnikov certainly conceals the great power and speed needed to achieve those stunning virtuoso feats — the *grands ballonnés,* those astounding leaps high up toward the rafters; the *cabrioles,* when his legs beat gracefully together in midair; and the *grands jetés,* those leaps where he barely seems to touch the ground before bounding up again.

No one can do them like he can.

He even combines a seemingly impossible series of movements, as in the *grand jeté en tournant battan.* Leaping high into the air, he turns 180 degrees; then, while moving backward with his legs leading, beats them together twice in a scissorlike motion before lightly landing.

And he makes it look so easy.

He understates the supreme effort with which he pulls off the seemingly impossible while retaining the correct, classroom ideal in the line of his body.

It is not usual for a male dancer to keep his classic line. It is more often dropped while jumping or moving.

The loss of the correct body position is a part of the style of the first kind of dancer, the dancer who lets the audience see the machinery, the bare bones of the movement, the muscles straining to achieve the *grand ballonné,* or the double *tour en l'air,* in which the dancer revolves two full turns in a blur of motion.

Most dancers do it in a blur of motion. Only Baryshnikov appears to slow it down. The air around him jells, supporting his body. He is buoyant.

It is all an illusion, of course. Gravity tugs at him just as strongly as it does at any other dancer, and it takes an incredible amount of power to make the movement seem so easy, so graceful, so controlled.

Audiences sympathetically strain when they see the dancer strain, and they applaud the fact of gravity so visibly overcome.

There is an emotional tie between the ballet audience and the dancer, just as there often is in the sports arena. People in the audience rise from their seats as the athlete skims over the bar in the high jump. They tense their arms and backs as they struggle with the weightlifter to set a new record. They mirror the tension in Bruce Jenner's face as he puts forth his utmost to win the decathlon championship.

The physical empathy is greater when the audiences can see the effort vividly displayed, but the intellectual awe is lacking. The line is less classic, less perfect. The magic is diluted.

In Baryshnikov's case, although he telegraphs the supreme power involved, the ease with which he executes the movements makes it seem as if he is hardly trying.

He floats — as that other famed dancer, Muhammad Ali, might say — like a butterfly.

And he always, always keeps his body in perfect line.

He projects both the emotion and the intellectual awe.

It is this rare ability that makes Baryshnikov unique. And this uniqueness has helped him propel dance to the unprecedented popularity it is currently enjoying in America.

In 1965, four years after Rudolf Nureyev astonished the West with his explosive, heroic style, the total dance audience in this country was estimated at one million.

Respectable, but still rather exclusive when spread among the many American dance companies.

But by 1972, two years before Baryshnikov came upon the scene, something had happened. The most popular event on campus was not a rock concert, nor a sports event; it was a dance performance. The national audience for dance had grown to eleven million.

And in 1978, the figure had reached fifteen million and was climbing. Why?

The fame of key ballet figures such as Baryshnikov helped, but people were also discovering that the ballet held all the excitement and splendor of the sports arena. Seething, at times, with a civilized and peaceful ferment. Also, there was usually a story line. The most popular ballets have a story line. And ballet had the appeal of art. Of beauty.

The ballet is the utmost extension of one of our most primitive instincts — the need to dance. From the caveman pounding his feet in a ritualized celebration of the hunt, through the rain dance of the American Indian, the days of jitterbugs, twisters, and disco junkies, to the perfection of Baryshnikov.

That's it!

How much farther can dance go?

Of course, not everyone takes to the ballet. Then again, not everyone takes to baseball, or football, or the opera, or great literature.

In his novel *Kalki,* Gore Vidal has one of his characters utter the philosophy of one who does not subscribe to a season at the ABT.

"Next to mime," Vidal's character says, "I hate ballet. If there is a hell being prepared for me, it will be an eternity of watching Marcel Marceau alternate with the Bolshoi Ballet."

And neither the ballet, Nureyev, Balanchine, nor Baryshnikov has made it into the closely packed 1450-plus pages of *The People's Almanac.* Apparently father and son, Wallace and Wallechinsky, did not believe ballet to be a part of the culture of The People.

They're right. Ballet is still not a part of America's popular culture. It may be someday; it's come a long way from the turn of the century when, for all practical purposes, it didn't exist. But it still has a long way to go before it's truly popular.

In the early 1900s ballet was in a decline in the West. But in Russia it grew and prospered. In 1909, the Ballets Russes traveled from Saint Petersburg to Paris and stunned European audiences. Delighted them.

More! They wanted more.

The Ballets Russes gave them more and dominated the art of ballet for the next two decades.

Among the fantastic dancers in the Ballet Russe was one Vaslav Nijinsky, the greatest male dancer of his time.

There were other good male dancers around, but none was so brilliant

UPI Photo

as Nijinsky. None was brilliant enough to eclipse the ballerinas of the day. But Nijinsky could.

Of Nijinsky, the sculptor Rodin said, "His beauty is that of antique fresco and sculpture; he is the ideal model, whom one longs to draw and sculpt."

At the time Rodin saw him, Nijinsky was performing in his controversial ballet *The Afternoon of a Faun.* Controversial because the critics found the choreography too erotic.

"When the curtain rises to reveal him reclining on the ground," continued Rodin, "one knee raised, the pipe at his lips, you would think him a statue; and nothing could be more striking than the impulse with which, at the climax, he lies face down on the secreted veil, kissing it and hugging it to him with passionate abandon."

Meeting for the first time at a December 1974 party, Nureyev and Baryshnikov prepare to kiss in the Russian tradition. The party marked Nureyev's opening on Broadway with his own dance company.

The ABT production of *The Nutcracker* is Misha's own version of the Petipa ballet, in which he danced with ballerina Marianna Tcherkassky and later with Gelsey Kirkland. It is a ballet of special significance for Kirkland, who reexperienced childhood dancing it and enjoys it immensely.

It was this scene that brought forth prurient thoughts and opened forbidden doors in the critics' minds. They were scandalized by the twelve-minute ballet, just as the Russian Ministry of Culture was upset by the seminude Baryshnikov bounding about the stage in *The Creation of the World,* fifty years later.

Let us stop for a moment to analyze something. To give you a small idea of what a polished performance entails, *The Afternoon of a Faun* takes only twelve minutes to present, but it requires 120 rehearsals to perfect.

It is little wonder that Baryshnikov calls dancing very hard work.

The Russians, after Nijinsky, continued to produce outstanding dancers, many of them male. In the West — where there was ballet at all — the female dancers, the ballerinas, held the spotlight.

Partially this reflected the stigma that ballet carried for a male dancer. Was a good all-American boy going to grow up to be a ballet dancer?

Never.

He could be a baseball player or a doctor, a lawyer or an Indian chief — well, maybe not an Indian chief — or he could be out crushing bones on the football field. He could perform high jumps at a track meet.

As a result of this stigma, men who did become dancers suffered from two handicaps. First, they usually began their study late, after their bodies had developed and the flexibility they needed for the dance was gone. And, second, they had to overact, to be very *macho,* to compensate for the feminine stigma that being a dancer carried.

They danced in boldly masculine ways.

Edward Villella, for example, was an athletic dancer. He sacrificed purity of line for the expression of power. Villella looked and danced like an athlete. And an athlete was — at that time — considered absolutely masculine, above the suspicion of sexual ambivalence.

Not until the Russians came to our shores once more — Nureyev in '61 and Baryshnikov in '74 — did this feeling begin to change. Their superb technique and limber bodies seemed to prove that the dance could be a respectable art for a man.

Rudolf Nureyev brought a male animal magnetism, a sensual quality, to dance. He wasn't above showing off, either. He hammed it up, extended his princelike personality beyond the theater stage. He had a regal, sculptured quality. Disdainful.

Also, he was a good dancer.

He didn't, though, have the "one of the guys" image that Baryshnikov possessed.

Rudy was royalty.

Misha was people.

When Baryshnikov showed up in New York — hitherto Nureyev territory — he was twenty-six. Nureyev was ten years older.

Rudolf was approaching the years when his dancing would be less athletic and more stylistic. This usually comes to a male dancer at around the age of forty. By forty-five, male dancers are moving into character roles.

Would the young Baryshnikov take the spotlight away from Nureyev? Could they be friends? Or would the competition between the two men, and their respective personalities and talents, stand in their way?

There is "no competition between us whatsoever," Baryshnikov said in 1974.

Misha called Nureyev "a very great dancer." He termed it an honor to be dancing in New York while Nureyev was also performing in the city.

Nureyev said flattering things about Baryshnikov. Then.

Nureyev also denied trying to dance better than anyone else, trying to turn their dancing into a competition. He competed only against himself.

Nureyev called Baryshnikov "an extremely talented dancer." And he wished him well, adding that he hoped Baryshnikov would absorb the great ballet riches of the West.

The two men became friends, and Baryshnikov stayed in Nureyev's home when he traveled to London.

But the friendship cooled. A little over a year later, in November 1975, Nureyev's evaluation of his fellow expatriate reflected this change.

Admitting that their relationship was not as close as it had been earlier, Nureyev reminded people that there were other dancers around — he named Fernando Bujones and Anthony Dowell. Baryshnikov, he said, was not the only great dancer.

Perhaps Baryshnikov was stealing too much of Nureyev's thunder. Or it may have been simply the difference in life styles and attitudes.

Offstage — as well as on — Nureyev was, or could be, outrageous. Flamboyant.

Baryshnikov was not.

Rudy was a jet-setter, a trend-setter, a confidant of the social set. He seemed to glow in the flash of the cameras.

Misha was quieter. Seemingly more serious. ("I am very serious. I am serious man, really.")

He was partial to faded jeans and patterned shirts. He gave interviews, but reluctantly.

He was happier when he was left alone.

The cooling friendship between Misha and Rudy may have been caused by the constant comparison to which the two Russian dancers from the Kirov had been subjected.

Liza Minnelli and Mikhail perform their own version of *Saturday Night Fever* at New York's celebrated Studio 54 in January 1978.

Things that Nureyev and Baryshnikov had in common were often cited. They were both perfectionists. They both took risks on stage. Yet, as Laurence Olivier once observed, nothing is really interesting in the theater unless the actor "risks sudden death."

To Baryshnikov, that was not quite true. He did not feel that the actor or dancer must think he is risking sudden death. Only the audience should feel that he is.

In any case, comparisons between Rudy and Misha pointed out their differences more than their similarities. For instance, in the ballet *Giselle,* Nureyev played the lead male role as it is usually interpreted. Albrecht, the count, was a cad.

Albrecht is aristocratic and authoritarian. In explaining how the role is usually interpreted, Baryshnikov called his social position and noble bearing the "most important aspects" of the role.

That is not the way he danced it.

He did not see Albrecht that way. Baryshnikov envisioned an Albrecht who was sincere. Who was a little naive, boyish. How else could the boyish Baryshnikov play it? And his Albrecht was innocently, thoroughly, in love.

In *Giselle,* the romantic ballet that premiered in Paris in 1841, Count Albrecht disguises himself as a peasant in order to win the favors of a beautiful peasant girl, Giselle. She falls in love with the Count, who keeps his nobility a secret from her.

Albrecht has a rival for Giselle's heart — Hilarion. Discovering who Albrecht really is, Hilarion jealously tries to break up the romance of the star-crossed lovers by revealing Albrecht's identity. And also revealing the fact that Albrecht is betrothed to another, a girl of his own class.

When Giselle learns the truth, she goes mad and dies. And because she has died before her wedding day, she has to join the Wilis, the restless spirits of unmarried maidens. But she saves her lover, Albrecht, from his romantic fate, to dance on for all eternity.

Giselle has been called "an old warhorse of a romantic ballet" and "a tearjerker." Whatever one might think of it, the ballet has become one of the most successful of all time.

Giselle was important to Baryshnikov because many people did not believe he could dance it. He was too young for the role. His short and slightly chunky body did not fit the streamlined image most people had of Albrecht.

He was nervous and tense during rehearsals for the ballet. He practiced daily with Natalia Makarova, who was his partner in the dance.

Unlike many other ballet stars, who conserve energy by walking through their steps in a rehearsal, Baryshnikov usually dances every step.

Many times, this is unintentional, he says, "but the dancing takes over."

He pulled it off. In New York, on July 27; 1974, he made the boyish Albrecht live.

He was outstanding. His technique was effortless, his acting superb. His performance was poetic.

One orchestra member was so overcome that she nearly threw her violin onstage. Like all the other members of the audience that night, she was entranced by a dancer who had set out to do his best — and had done so.

What is the essence of all art? It is "to have pleasure in giving pleasure," says Baryshnikov.

Pleasure he has given. And pleasure he has received in return.

But, at times, he hates the dance.

When?

"After a bad performance." But this happens very rarely and his hatred of his work never lasts long.

Baryshnikov insists that he dances because he is happy. To him, the dance is "a light, giddy chill in my guts."

He still thrills to the applause as he did that first time in the Latvian school, but no matter how much applause and how many bravos he receives, there are always doubts that gnaw at his mind. Could he have done better? Was the heart-stopping *brisé* — the spectacular leg beats in the air that he has done so well — a personal affectation, or did it belong in the ballet?

He worries about the impression he has made after a performance. For the interpretation is his, even though the step is in the ballet. He calls it the "last gasp of the soul."

Whatever.

Who, other than a ballet master, could argue the point?

The first ballet created for him in the West was choreographed by John Butler to Samuel Barber's music. *Medea* was a dance full of frenzy, a dance of vengeance, a duet with Carla Fracci first performed in 1975 at Italy's Festival of Two Worlds in Spoleto.

The ballet combines both classic and modern steps, and it was the first ballet in which Baryshnikov performed not wearing tights. He found it fascinating and exciting. He had danced into the modern era, into the twenty-first century.

Finally.

He is very excited about roles that are created for him. He feels that they open up new and unrealized worlds.

Naturally, he has gained from dancing the classical repertory. But he longs to dance in ballets by Robbins, Balanchine, Tudor, MacMillan, and Petit. He wants to work with choreographers who believe he can dance in their ballets. He is willing to grant the choreographer the right over everything when the ballet is being created.

It was Baryshnikov in the classics that the audiences loved, but they would learn to appreciate his work in modern ballets, too. For, as Clive Barnes pointed out, he was born to dance everything.

"He dances like the wind of heaven."

He did dance in practically everything. Running through Tudor, Butler, Petit, Tharp, Tetley, Balanchine, and others. Sixteen new works were created for him. He mastered thirty new roles of varying scope. In just two years. He even worked freelance, in such numbers as *Pas de Duke* with Judith Jamison at Alvin Ailey's American Dance Theater. His freelance fees as an international star have brought him $10,000 for each performance.

He excelled in Twyla Tharp's *Push Comes to Shove,* a funny potpourri of jazz, disco, and classical ballet. He felt that the point of performing in such modern works was to see more. It would open doors for him, would aid him in adding new depths to his already fathomless style.

He was especially interested in doing ballets that incorporated the Martha Graham mode of dancing. He didn't know that school of dancing. And Alvin Ailey used it.

He worried about "all the contractions in the stomach" that Ailey wanted. He felt he couldn't do them well. Yet he was willing to try because it was an interesting situation for him.

He found it difficult to combine his classical training with the quick jazz steps and confessed that at first he felt like "a cow."

Antony Tudor also presented a challenge for him. Here the challenge was mental, not technical. He had to know exactly what he was dancing about. Not simply think it on stage. Know it.

Baryshnikov never forgets that the dancer is performing for an audience. He knows how important it is not to forget that.

He realizes his dancing is not disco dancing. He is not dancing only for himself. He must dance to the ballet and to the audience.

In Russia, the connection with the theater and the audience was strong. He could understand their reaction. He knew how they would like certain things, what other dancers would say. He also hoped they would like what he did.

Or at least, he hoped, they would not hate it.

Even with a great artist, there are sometimes uncertainties. There is a need for approval.

As an artist, Baryshnikov prefers ballets with a good dramatic plan. Be-

Photograph © Lois Greenfield

cause of this, he likes ballets with a good story.

Even so, he is not enamored of *Swan Lake,* one of the most famous ballets. Nevertheless, he did like Erik Bruhn's production of the ballet. Siegfried had more scenes than in any other version and Bruhn made the prince a much more active participant in the drama.

Baryshnikov danced in Bruhn's production in Canada in September 1975, with Nadia Potts.

Bruhn remembers when Baryshnikov came to the National Ballet of Canada in 1975. It was there that he danced his first *Swan Lake.* Bruhn taught him the role of the Prince in his production of the ballet. All the while he coached him in the role, he found it hard to believe that he had actually danced the role himself. "Did I really do that?" he kept thinking. He had completely disassociated himself from a character he had por-

The classicist Baryshnikov was especially interested in learning the Martha Graham mode of dancing. Alvin Ailey used it for *Pas de Duke,* for which Misha danced free-lance with Judith Jamison.

When dancing in Ailey's flashy, fun *Pas de Duke*, Baryshnikov worried about "all those contractions in the stomach." He couldn't do them well. He lacked the smooth fluidity that Jamison brought to the dance, he felt, and confessed that he sometimes looked like a cow. But the jazzy, blues construction captured his imagination and his performance was beautiful and poetic.

trayed often. He calls it an "odd sensation" but also a "relief."

Baryshnikov says that he would probably never have danced in *Swan Lake* had he stayed in the Soviet Union. He didn't care for the Kirov presentation of the ballet. He thought it too massive and grand. He also felt that the role of Siegfried had a tendency to get lost. Baryshnikov prefers a role that is central to the ballet; he doesn't care for one that is "just a prop."

It's not that he disagrees with choreographers who stress the role of the male dancer as a lifter of the ballerinas.

To a point, he believes in this approach. But he also believes that the role of the male dancer — in order to be a good role — must be essential to the plot.

He has been lucky in his selection of dance partners. Gelsey Kirkland and Natalia Makarova are splendid examples. Baryshnikov calls them "great individuals." His relationships with each ballerina have been different — the mental contact, the physical situation. It has been "very exciting for me," Baryshnikov says in tribute to the ballerinas.

"And I hope," he adds, "for them, too."

Undoubtedly.

Once, joking, he said that the only qualification he looked for in a partner was that she didn't step on his toes. Then, relenting somewhat in this severe restriction, he said he might even overlook that if, when she did, she said, "Sorry." An urchin grin lit up his face.

His partners are good even when they dance with others, but ABT director Lucia Chase says, "Everybody dances better when he's around."

When Misha first came to America, he had no plans to do his own productions, especially not to choreograph them. It was difficult enough to dance and do ballet. Also, he felt that great dancers do not always make great choreographers. The reverse was also true, he said.

But he found that it was not all that difficult after all. Although he still did not consider himself a choreographer, merely a restager or producer. He worked on a Baryshnikov version of *The Nutcracker,* which was presented nationally over CBS-TV, and a shortened, Broadway-type version of a Russian favorite, *Don Quixote.*

He called *Don Q.* "a mess," but added, "I love it."

Baryshnikov was not the first to fiddle with the choreography of the Petipa ballet. The version he tackled was an oft-tampered-with one. Through the years, dancers and choreographers have added or taken away something from the original until it has become more of less a showcase of dancers' specialties.

Although based on the Cervantes tale of the errant knight and his faithful companion, they are incidental characters to the plot. The story, essentially, is that of the lusty barber Basilio, and his pursuit of Kitri, the innkeeper's daughter.

Don Q. is noted for its uproarious comedy, its drama, and its many folk sequences. And it contains some excellent virtuoso passages for the principal dancers.

If the ballet is as much of a mess as Baryshnikov claims, why did he bother with this "crazy Russian salad of a ballet?"

Anticipating the question, he asked reporters if they had wondered why he had bothered to stage it.

It was not a great ballet, yet Russians adore it.

Well produced, Baryshnikov added, the ballet had "style, charm, and a genuine atmosphere." He liked it, too, because it demanded more than academic technique, and it assuredly demanded that. A successful *Don Quixote*, according to Baryshnikov, demanded "stage presence, mimetic ability, and comic flair."

He starred in his own production and succeeded admirably, since he possessed all the necessary qualifications for success, especially the "comic flair." He has a natural ability to play the clown, which he has displayed in unaffected delight in other ballets, including *Push Comes to Shove.*

Maybe this is not great ballet, but it is fun, and in the way Misha restaged it as "classic vaudeville," the fun is enhanced.

He cut it and edited it in such a way that it was as well paced as a Broadway show. He shaped it to conform to what he believed was "American taste."

Whether or not he succeeded in his intention is a matter for the critics and audiences to decide — or for posterity. But it was a lively, enjoyable, fast-paced version.

But he had had enough of producing for a while. After *Don Quixote,* he planned no more Baryshnikov productions. He wanted to dance for a while, in different ballets. In a different company.

Dancing is a necessity for him. When he is not working, he feels "off balance." He works hard, in the realization that life is short. He will relax later. When? "When I stop dancing."

When he was dancing at the Kirov, he spent most of his time dancing nineteenth-century ballets. After he came to America and the ABT, he still spent a lot of time in those ballets. Finally, it was enough.

In April 1978, he announced that he would henceforth be dancing with Balanchine's City Ballet.

He had wanted to work with the master choreographer, Balanchine, from the beginning.

Now he had made his move.

Push Comes to Shove is a serious dance, says the number-one fan of choreographer Tharp. In it she so integrates the music with the movements that everything is logical and beautiful. Tharp, Misha says, is a "genius," and he felt he had never worked so hard to learn a dance. It was to him as if he went "to the moon and back again." With Misha in *Push Comes to Shove* are Clark Tippet, left, and Marianna Tcherkassky.

Back Home
En Arrière

I want to dance in Balanchine ballets."
Baryshnikov spoke those words not long after he made his great leap to the West in 1974. But instead of landing at the City Ballet with Balanchine, he placed his feet firmly on the stage of the American Ballet Theatre and made a four-year stopover.

Nevertheless, those words kept echoing through rehearsal halls; he could not shake the intensity of the thought; the idea continued to haunt him, daring him.

Finally he had to do it. He had to join Balanchine's company.

He had dreamed of joining for a long time. But he held back. He wasn't sure of Balanchine's reaction. He did not want to be a dancer the choreographer didn't want to have.

The desire may have always been there, and Baryshnikov may have stated many, many times that he wanted more than anything in the world to dance in Balanchine ballets. Nevertheless, the move astonished the dance world.

Rocked it, some said.

Should those fans who want to see him dance in the classics buy tickets to the New York City Ballet? No. "Go see *The Turning Point*," he says.

Why had Baryshnikov done it? Why had he traded fame and fortune for the fragile honor of dancing for the master?

It definitely wasn't for money. His earnings at City Ballet would be far less than the $3,500 a performance he was getting at the ABT. Salaries at City Ballet run more like $750 a *week*.

That's quite a pay cut.

Then, maybe he doesn't need money now. Maybe he has enough money. After all, when you earn more than $200,000 a year, maybe you just aren't all that interested in making more money.

Baryshnikov, echoing the past, called it an artistic decision. It was the same sentiment he had used in explaining his defection from the Soviet Union four years earlier.

The decision was a long time brewing, but it went from simmer to boil as he became bored with what he was doing, and more and more appreciative of Balanchine's work.

Misha called Balanchine's ballets "very wonderful" no matter how they were danced. "I need his choreography more than it needs me," Misha said in 1976, two years before he made his momentous decision.

After the April announcement he indicated the depth of his boredom with non-Balanchine ballets. He related how tired he was of ballets in which he was merely on display, ones in which critics had nothing more to write about than the shape he was in.

He had begun to have little talks with himself. "To be, or not to be," as in *Hamlet*.

"I decided to be," says Baryshnikov.

The decision was all Misha's. Balanchine did not beg him to join.

Balanchine denied casting any lures at Baryshnikov. He said that Misha just wanted to dance with their company. Like everyone else. At one time Nureyev had expressed a wish to dance with City Ballet, to do *Giselle* and *Swan Lake*. Balanchine had said, "When you get tired of them, then you come here."

But Nureyev never got tired.

Balanchine felt that it was too expensive for Nureyev and Baryshnikov to go to City Ballet. They don't pay anything compared to other companies. Balanchine had come from the same place as Rudy and Misha and he had never made any money. Even when he worked on Broadway. He could see that the two great dancers must first make some money, dancing everywhere. If they did not, they would starve in the ballet world.

Was that what Baryshnikov had set out to do? Make his bundle and then be an "artist"?

Who could blame him if that were true?

But it wasn't.

The reason he did not join Balanchine immediately, he said, was because he was "emotionally upset and bewildered."

He did not know what to do.

It was Natalia Makarova — a woman he had known for ten years — who invited him to join the ABT. And he was grateful for the marvelous opportunity. But as soon as he performed for the ABT, he felt it was too late to join the City Ballet. Because Mr. Balanchine wouldn't be first.

Baryshnikov also needed to look around. He wanted to scout out the territory and see just what was happening. He had to make sure that he understood Balanchine's point of view about dancing.

He had once asked Balanchine about dancing his ballets in Europe. Balanchine reminded him, not without irony, that his public expected him to do the "glamorous thing."

Baryshnikov felt that Balanchine was telling him to do his thing and let Balanchine do his.

The public does expect Baryshnikov to do his "glamorous thing." Many fans will be disappointed with the Baryshnikov who will be performing at top speed, executing the sharp, quick footwork in the abstract City Ballet productions.

Balanchine's choreography is difficult. That fact alone should present enough excitement to appease the high-priced ticketholders. But it probably won't. Not all of them, anyway.

Does Baryshnikov really care if they are appeased?

No.

He wants to dance in Balanchine's ballets. When he does, the audience will know what they are going to see. To that part of the public that is disappointed at not seeing him in *Don Quixote* or *Giselle,* Baryshnikov says, "Don't come."

Perhaps they can see him in *The Turning Point.*

At the American Ballet Theatre, the dancers are more important than the ballets. At the New York City Ballet, it is the opposite. Popular recognition and money are offered to ABT stars. The City Ballet offers far less in concrete terms, but for Baryshnikov, it is far more. It is the chance to work with the master.

The master and his new student share a common ballet legacy. George Balanchine, a native of Saint Petersburg, graduated from the Imperial Maryinsky Ballet School and joined the Maryinsky Ballet. That was in 1921, before the Maryinsky's name was changed to Kirov and Saint Petersburg became Leningrad.

Both men started from the same gate.

"We went through the same school," Balanchine acknowledges. "He

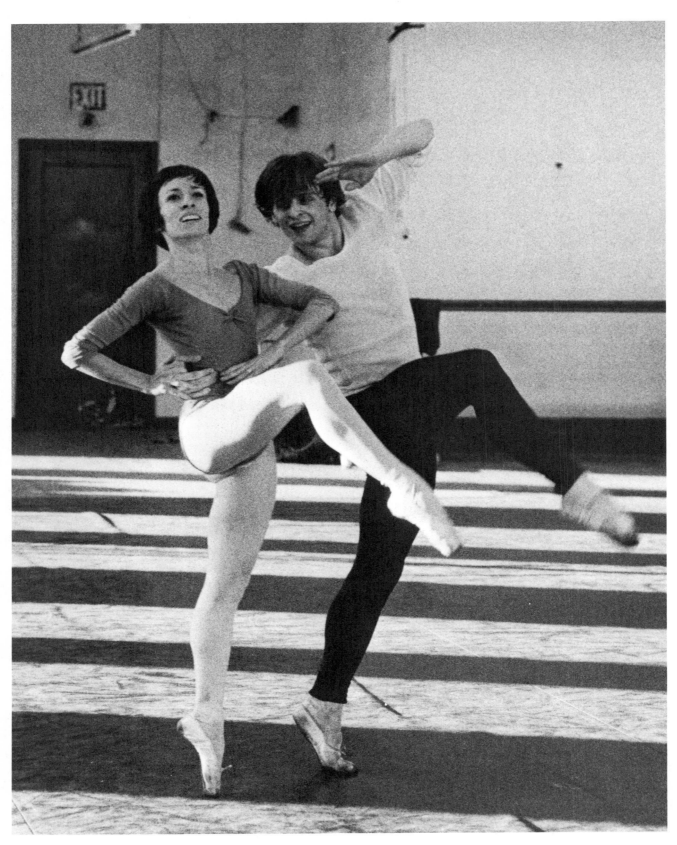

Christine Sarry and Baryshnikov in rehearsal (above) and in a performance of Feld's *Variations on America*, a seven-minute romp, full of vitality and good humor.

Photograph © Lois Greenfield

The score for *Variations on America*, originally a Charles Ives organ fantasia, was orchestrated by William Schuman. It is, Feld said, "a series of opinions" full of optimism. Performed in March 1977 by Sarry and Baryshnikov, the ballet demands speed and lucidity because of its incredible compression. It is, after all, two hundred years of history presented in seven minutes—an apple-pie, blue-eyed, sunny look at America.

Photograph © Lois Greenfield

likes to point his feet and do beats. It's all very classical.''

When he made the change in ballet companies, Baryshnikov became the first dancer from the Soviet Union to join Balanchine's company. He feels that this move is a homecoming of sorts. It will be like going back to the Kirov. Back to the 200-year-old Russian tradition of ballet.

In Russia ballet education is a very serious business. The focus is on classical ballet, mime, and character dancing. Dancers in the West come from many kinds of schools — private classes, New York City ballet schools, and schools in remote parts of the country. Each teacher has a different background and point of view. Many different versions of classical ballet are taught — Danish, Italian, French, and new American. The Russians have but one discipline, and education in the dance in Russia is not informal.

"I am going back," Baryshnikov says of his move to Balanchine, "and still going forward."

Going back because Balanchine's base is one of strict classicism. Going forward because Balanchine has refined and polished his ballets to such a degree that they have been transformed from classical to modern. They stress speed, agility, and a startling angularity. The music evokes the dance. Movement is everything. The story, if any, is incidental. But the underlying form is pure.

It is, Misha says, classical dance in the great Russian tradition of Petipa. But Balanchine has developed a new kind of ballet theater, one that never existed before.

But, Baryshnikov adds, the flow of the choreography at the City Ballet is such that there is no preparation for movements. In the standard nineteenth-century ballets, there is time to prepare.

Gelsey Kirkland has commented on this difference. She should know. She did what Baryshnikov has done, only in reverse. First to Balanchine, then to the ABT. If you watch Baryshnikov before he jumps, she says, then slow down a film of the jump, you will see that it's almost like a pole vaulter's jump. The natural power of the torso is being used.

He won't be doing that anymore.

Although Misha enjoyed working with modern choreographers such as Alvin Ailey and Twyla Tharp, he felt for the past year or so that the work was becoming repetitious. It was tiring to go through the same routines he has been through for twelve years.

It will certainly be a change for him. The New York City Ballet is a special world with special laws and a special philosophy.

Baryshnikov declares it "a privilege" to work with Balanchine. He calls himself, and happily so, an "instrument" in Balanchine's hands.

It was in April of 1978 that Balanchine and Baryshnikov sat down together to seriously discuss the change. They met in Balanchine's apartment.

Baryshnikov had signaled the meeting, had made overtures. Balanchine responded with the invitation to his apartment and it was settled.

The settlement amounted to this: There would be no special allowances made for the star. If he wanted to join, he had to join permanently. "We don't have guest artists," Balanchine said.

After one year, Baryshnikov would be free to leave. Dancers who sign contracts with Balanchine sign for a year at a time. They are not made to feel they are in prison. Free to go, they usually stay.

"I'm glad that he's coming," Balanchine confesses. He is very pleased. Not because he is getting a superstar, but because he is getting a dancer.

Although Baryshnikov can appear as a guest star elsewhere, just as any other dancer from Balanchine's company can, he will not be dancing with other ballet companies in New York City.

And there is an acknowledged "no-star" policy at the NYCB. But that hardly perturbs superstar Baryshnikov.

"I never called myself a star," he says. "I'm a dancer."

He realizes it won't be easy for him, but he feels that he can find himself in Balanchine's choreography. He hopes to find a new attitude toward the public, a new aspect of his entire professional life.

He does not want to talk about what he is giving up. He would rather discuss what he is getting.

Was it true, as rumors suggested, that Balanchine was looking for a successor? Balanchine is seventy-four, and although immortal in one sense, he is certainly mortal in another. Is he planning to groom Baryshnikov to be his successor? It seems unlikely.

But Baryshnikov will be getting the benefit of years of experience from one of the founders of twentieth-century dance. Perhaps only Martha Graham has exerted as much influence on modern dance as has Balanchine.

The City Ballet also has some excellent dancers — Edward Villella, Peter Martins, Patricia McBride, and the upcoming Heather Watts, to name a few — and a wonderful repertory of ballets.

No one knows what form ballet will take a quarter of a century from now. *Giselle* and *Swan Lake* will probably still be around, but for the rest it is hard to say.

Balanchine, along with Jerome Robbins, has inspired a whole generation of choreographers. Their influence will undoubtedly be felt. Which of them will be the most influential? No one can know for sure. Not too many new young choreographers are around. Beyond Balanchine's and Robbins's works, which will survive, the future is uncertain.

Jerome Robbins, who also made the shift from the ABT to the City Ballet, was not surprised to hear of Baryshnikov's decision to join them.

He called City Ballet a "serious company" and saw it as a place for "serious artists."

Neither was Natalia Makarova shocked. She cited the artistic growth all great dancers seek. She could understand and respect that desire. She felt that the ABT had become routine for Baryshnikov.

But Makarova felt that nobody could replace him at the ABT. "Misha is Misha," she said.

She did not know if she could have done the same thing. She is not ready to separate herself from the classics. She needs them, she said, emotionally. And the "exclusive" policy that the NYCB demands seems strange to her.

Russian artists who made leaps to the West thought they would have total artistic freedom. But they reckoned without ballet politics. For example, they learned they could not dance with both the ABT and the New York City Ballet. They wonder why. They cannot understand why Balanchine does not ask them to join his company even for one season. They do not see how this could hurt anything.

But, all that aside, Makarova is happy for Misha. She feels he knows what he is doing. And dancing the wonderful Balanchine and Robbins ballets will "certainly enrich his art."

Whatever happens to Baryshnikov, his presence at the NYCB will not affect the company.

"Why should it?" Balanchine asks. Baryshnikov will merely be an additional member, one very good new dancer for the company. When so many get sick, "it's good to have someone healthy."

How quickly will Misha fit into the company?

Balanchine will decide what ballets will be good for Misha. And what ballets Misha will do well in.

Baryshnikov danced gloriously in the company's Saratoga, New York, summer season in July 1978, after being with Balanchine for only a few weeks.

What the future will bring for both Misha and the City Ballet is an intriguing question. Will City Ballet, for instance, have to put up signs saying "Misha tickets all sold out," as the ABT did? Can a "no-star" policy really hide the glow of Baryshnikov's superstardom?

And would Gelsey Kirkland, who left Balanchine to dance with Baryshnikov, return to the fold?

The answer to that last question, at least, was supplied by "Mr. B."

"She is not coming," he said. "She can stay where she is."

Did he actually say that? Or was he misquoted? Gelsey does not feel

Photograph © Lois Greenfield

that sounded like Balanchine. She wonders exactly what he said. She cannot believe he would hold what she did against her.

In any case, Gelsey is contented where she is. "I know this is where I want to be."

That doesn't mean, though, that she has lost any respect for either Balanchine or his ballets. She admits that when she sees a "glorious Balanchine ballet," she wants to get up and dance it. But the new ballets she has danced have become a part of her. She is happy.

Baryshnikov wants the ballets to become a part of him, too.

He is now thirty. At thirty-five, he feels the change would come too late. Even at thirty-two.

He knows he is still young and "quick to learn new things."

And, as Gelsey Kirkland once remarked, "Working with first-class people makes you more first-class yourself."

Old friend Natalia Makarova is happy for Misha. Dancing the Balanchine ballets will "enrich his art." But nobody can replace him at the ABT. "Misha is Misha."

Frank Sinatra sings (on record) for Twyla Tharp's *Once More, Frank.* Here she dances her own choreography with Misha. Twyla created the ballet for the two of them for a special ABT gala performance. It was a unique experience for Misha to be in a ballet in which the choreographer also danced.

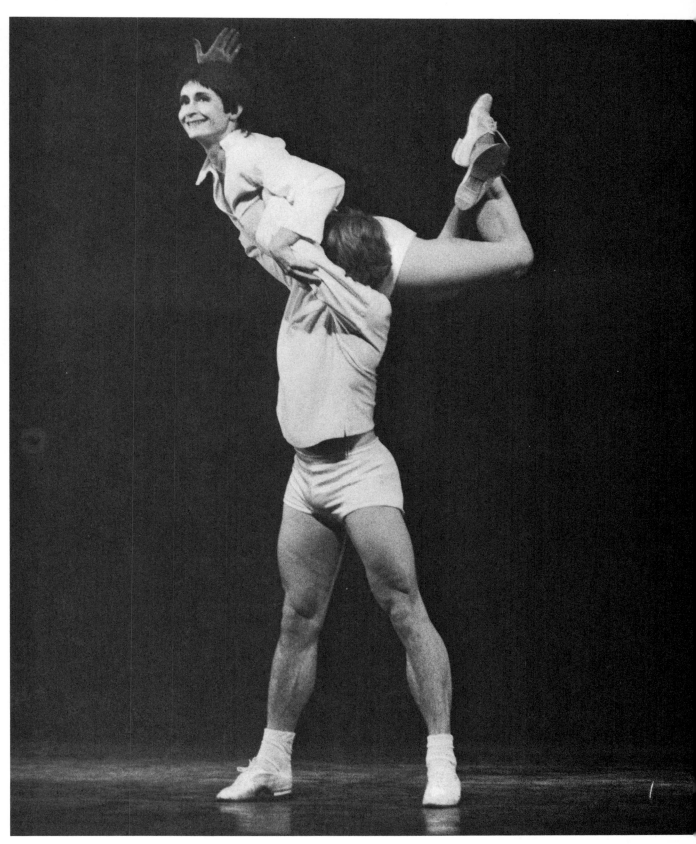

Time,
Pain, and Stress
Coda

He's thirty now.

At twenty-nine he gave himself only six or seven more years of dancing on the stage.

After that he did not know what he would do. He knew that his body was stiffer, stronger, and not as flexible as a ballerina's body. Also, he had jumped and expended much more energy than a ballerina.

When a male dancer reaches the age of thirty-five, his muscles no longer respond as readily. That's when the real pressure begins.

Thirty, in professional dance terms, is like fifty in ordinary terms. It's also true for athletes, especially those who are in sports that demand great physical stamina and strain. But, for dancers, the stress increases not only from wear and tear and age, but also from choreographers who are busy devising new ballets that are more demanding physically.

Baryshnikov does not plan to kill himself. "When it will be natural, I stop without regret," he once said.

He paraphrases a popular cigarette commercial of a few years back:

The tremendous physical stress on a dancer's body is similar to that on an athlete's. All the hazards that plague the sports star haunt the ballet idol.

"It's not how long you make it, it's how you make it . . . and what."

Again like an athlete, a dancer can burn himself out before his time if he doesn't take care of his body. He has to be constantly in training; a short layoff can hurt the performance. The dancer must keep in top shape at all times.

Dancers are, without a doubt, the "best-conditioned athletes," dancer Ted Kivitt states. If they skip practice for a week, they are totally out of shape.

Ted was thirty-two when Misha entered the ranks of the ABT. It was likely that Baryshnikov took some of the glow from Kivitt's career at the time. Ted thinks so.

But it didn't keep him from dancing, and dancing well. It simply took away some of the spotlight, some of the recognition. Ted is now in the prime of his dancing. Actually, he's at the end of his prime. Being realistic at thirty-six, he is appraising the future.

He admits that age is hard on male dancers. But there are parts for older men, parts that have a certain maturity about them. And dancing character roles often requires more technique.

Nevertheless, he claims the best insurance against too early an old age is to take good care of yourself.

There is, of course, no real insurance against the ravages of age.

And so age, sprains, twisted backs — all the hazards that plague an athlete — haunt the dancer. Even dancers with as much stamina as Baryshnikov.

In his first year in the West there was much pressure, which may have accounted for a lot of injuries. Since then he has learned a lot and his body protects itself mechanically. As he says, "I'm trying to survive."

A great many more performances are demanded of a star principal in the United States than in Russia. There, a dancer would perform maybe five times a month. Here, it could be as many as five times a week.

Besides performing, dancers like Baryshnikov take a daily ninety-minute ballet class. And if he is preparing for a new ballet, he will have to rehearse as much as six or seven hours a day. The schedule is altered on the day of the performance. An hour of rest is planned before the curtain goes up.

Even if he is completely exhausted after a performance, twelve hours later he must rehearse for a new role. His body has little chance to recuperate. At times he feels terrible, even with massages.

If he dances two ballets in one evening, he must have ten hours' sleep. A half day later he must be ready for his next rehearsal. Sometimes he performs on the same day he rehearses for another ballet the day after. You can "go bananas," Baryshnikov says.

UPI Photo

Misha usually gets one free day a month. He spends it either sleeping or fishing.

Anything to ease the pressure on his body.

In January 1975, while on a tour of Australia, he seriously strained a tendon in his ankle. He was able to finish the *pas de deux* from *Don Quixote,* which he was dancing with Natalia Makarova. But after two curtain calls, he passed out.

The ankle caused him pain long after he was allowed out of bed and had cast off his crutches.

At the time of the injury, he admitted he was "running on nervous energy." He said he was working on relieving that situation.

But he was just entering his new life, he was not there yet. With no set schedule and no organization, only nervous energy sustained him.

President Carter joined Washington's elite at the premiere of Baryshnikov's *Don Quixote*. Misha was "superb," said Carter, but Gelsey Kirkland got the kiss.

Later that year, he had begun to adapt, and was "asking for more and more performances."

As Baryshnikov has discovered often, the stress that a dancer can impose on his body is tremendous. And it can lead to injury.

Greg Osborne, twenty-three, an aspiring soloist at the ABT, knows both the bad and the good sides of dance training. He began studying ballet when he was ten. It wasn't because he was hooked on the dance; he did it for therapy. When he was nine he broke both his legs in a childhood accident. He had to wear the casts for six months, and the leg muscles had weakened. The following fall he went into ballet. Dance can be excellent physical therapy.

Since then, except for the usual sprains and strains, the only major injury he has experienced was a knee injury that resulted from a heavy schedule. He had been running from class to rehearsal to performance, "trying to do everything at once." He didn't warm up properly one evening and still tried to do the performance full-out. He hurt his knee.

He was out for two weeks, and it took six weeks before he could feel at ease when dancing. He danced most of the six weeks, but "very, very carefully."

How soon an injured dancer can dance again depends on the injury. Many dancers resume quickly without hurting themselves.

But there is pain. Dancers deal with pain all the time.

Edward Villella says that male dancers are under as much pressure as any athlete. The strength required to get through a six-minute *pas de deux* is greater than that needed for four rounds of boxing.

When Baryshnikov arrived in Washington, D.C., in April 1978 for the first performance of his *Don Quixote,* he was drained. His energy had been sapped by a hard seventeen-week tour. Besides directing and starring in the ballet, he had to attend company production meetings that lasted until three in the morning. Schedules were off; everyone was running, working at a frenetic pace. Still, the first full run-through of the ballet took place only two days before the premiere.

American ballet is demanding.

But to relax is difficult. Misha realizes that. He knows it is important to schedule things sensibly and not to overdo. But he likens himself to a horse that is used to pulling a great load. He can't begin to imagine what would happen if he stopped dancing.

He tries hard not to think about a future without the dance. He called the stage "a form of opium" for him. He must have it. He cannot do without it.

It was during that hectic Washington season that the Kitri of the evening, ballerina Martine van Hamel, fell on stage and injured her leg. It was

Santa Fe Saga, **with its Mexican-flavored score, gave Baryshnikov a multiplicity of character roles to perform in the high-stepping ballet.**

twenty minutes into the performance.

Fortunately, Baryshnikov was in the audience. He located his partner, Gelsey Kirkland, at a restaurant, and called her back to the theater. Together, she and Baryshnikov finished the performance.

Gelsey has also had her share of physical troubles. One time was at the Balanchine company, when she was given the chance to dance *Theme and Variations*. Balanchine had revised it and made it even more intricate than it had been.

Although she danced beautifully, the pressure of doing the steps caused her to develop tendonitis.

She loves dancing more than anything in the world, but she could not dance with the pain.

Dancing ballet is unnatural for the body. Toes are bruised, ankles are twisted, small bones are cracked. But, as Gelsey points out, as unnatural as dancing is, "you have to find a natural way of doing the unnatural."

Some dancers manage to do this better than others. The ones who do are given the credit they deserve.

Americans are a people in motion and they admire fitness, as Charles Fischl, general manager of the Atlanta Ballet, once remarked. People who recognize ballet as grueling admire its athletic side.

Maybe it's because of this intense, unrelenting pressure that many ballet dancers live in such a closed-off world; a world that could magnify psychological stresses. Again, something that the ballet dancer shares with the athlete.

Mark Spitz trained for twelve years to become an Olympic champion. And although he realized his ambition, he lost something in the pro-

Set in a frontier town of the Old West, *Santa Fe Saga* transformed the classical ballet star into a swaggering, macho cowboy, an Indian scout, an aristocratic badman, and a Mexican peasant. It was not the best ballet he had ever danced, but it was one of the liveliest.

cess — a social ease away from the pool and the competition. He was less well equipped than he might have been to meet the majority of the world that lives on dry land.

Dancers have a similar problem.

Many of them live as if they were locked inside a box. That is their world and they know nothing outside it. "I try not to be like that," says Edward Villella.

The day never ends for a dancer.

If he goes to a dinner party, he restricts himself to one drink, maybe two. He can't drink too much because his next role is always a demanding one. And before he can dance it, he must plan the many things directly associated with the dancing. Nevertheless, he is a happy man, both in his professional and personal life. He feels "very privileged" to be able to do what he likes to do.

Even Baryshnikov, for all his periods of gloom and his tendency to moan, "It's impossible," goes on. And does the impossible.

He recognizes that there is a time in a young artist's life when he must bring something of himself to the stage, something deep from within. And it must be there to begin with if he is to bring it out. Performers who are well trained but not morally disciplined fall apart.

Baryshnikov has also been heard to mutter about "the moral preparation" he has to endure in the perfection of a new role.

He says he is not yet a dancer. He is in the process of becoming. He is still learning.

He admits he has made many mistakes. But they are his mistakes. He has planned his life, sometimes refusing to do things, and being right about his refusal. And sometimes refusing to do things, and being wrong.

He feels he must manage his life. It would be "terrible" at the end to say, "My God! This fellow who was responsible for my life. He was wrong."

He trusts his own taste more than that of others. He conducts his own life. When he is wrong he is free to say, "Is your mistake, you stupid dummy." He is talking to himself.

It takes a special kind of person to be a dancer. They have to give up much. But a talented, dedicated dancer such as Mikhail Baryshnikov gains a lot also. Fame, fortune, respect, the sense of fulfillment that comes from achieving what you dreamed of, and the indescribable joy of being able to earn your living by doing what you love to do most of all.

Misha has that.

What else could anyone ask?

"Health." He is serious. Just for a moment.

"And also," he grins, "a good lunch."

The 1978 *Dance Magazine* award was presented to a clowning Baryshnikov by a delighted Judith Jamison. The award, given to Jamison in 1972, honors the top creative talent in the field of dance.

Index